Selling Services

T0309225

More than ever, our economy relies on the service industries – but selling services is far different from selling tangible products.

This book demystifies the selling of intangibles and teaches the required skills to grow any professional service business. Leveraging his 30 years' experience, leading sales expert Clifton Warren offers 26 lessons to help readers navigate the selling of complex and intangible solutions. Each chapter covers an important concept from A (Accountability) to Z (Zigzagging) in a concise and readable format, including a "to-do" action list that makes the book both a workbook and a study guide. By successfully applying the steps discussed in each chapter, professionals will substantially improve their performance and results, and anyone looking to drill down into specific topics will find additional resources to explore.

B2B sales professionals in banking, insurance, finance, and other services, and small business owners such as lawyers, architects, and engineers, as well as professionals transitioning into sales roles, will appreciate the thorough and easy-to-follow guidance that this book provides.

Clifton Warren is the principal of Clifton Warren Consulting. His firm trains professionals to market, sell, and win new clients across Australia, New Zealand, and the United States. He is the author of three books: *Financial Services Sales Handbook*, *Cross-Selling Financial Services*, and *Rain Maker Pro*. His monthly newsletter and podcast attract professionals globally. He holds a master's degree in business administration from Henley Management College, London and is a certified management consultant. Originally from California, he lives in Melbourne, Australia.

Selling Services

The ABC of Professional Selling

Clifton Warren

Routledge
Taylor & Francis Group

NEW YORK AND LONDON

Designed cover image: Getty

First published 2024
by Routledge
605 Third Avenue, New York, NY 10158

and by Routledge
4 Park Square, Milton Park, Abingdon, Oxon, OX14 4RN

Routledge is an imprint of the Taylor & Francis Group, an informa business

Library of Congress Cataloging-in-Publication Data
Names: Warren, Clifton T., author.
Title: Selling services: the ABC of professional selling / Clifton Warren.
Description: New York: Routledge, 2024. |
Includes bibliographical references and index.
Identifiers: LCCN 2023015188 (print) | LCCN 2023015189 (ebook) |
ISBN 9781032428567 (hardback) | ISBN 9781032428536 (paperback) |
ISBN 9781003364580 (ebook)
Subjects: LCSH: Selling. | Business planning. | Consultants–Marketing.
Classification: LCC HF5438.25 .W28617 2024 (print) |
LCC HF5438.25 (ebook) | DDC 658.8/1–dc23/eng/20230330
LC record available at https://lccn.loc.gov/2023015188
LC ebook record available at https://lccn.loc.gov/2023015189

ISBN: 9781032428567 (hbk)
ISBN: 9781032428536 (pbk)
ISBN: 9781003364580 (ebk)

DOI: 10.4324/9781003364580

Typeset in Optima
by Newgen Publishing UK

Rene "Fingers" Warren and Jordan T. Warren

Contents

Acknowledgments

I've had the opportunity to work, observe, and learn from scores of top sales professionals and colleagues from around the world – I'm continually learning from you everyday.

I'd like to thank the hundreds of clients and professionals from across Australia, New Zealand, Asia, and the United States who have placed their trust in me to help them improve their capabilities.

During the writing of this book I interviewed several top professionals who shared their success and methods, including Robert Kelly, CEO, Steadfast; Bernie McIntosh, Managing Director, Victorian Mortgage Group; Joe Arena, CEO, Procurement Australia; Simon Swanston, CEO, ClearView; Allan Manning, Founder and Chairman, LMI Group; Richard Crawford, CEO, Community Broker Network; Ward Dedman, CEO, EBM Insurance; Mark Anderson, Barrister and Legal Risk Specialist; Kathleen Beck, Mortgage Banker, Doorway Home Loans; and Kylie Stephens, Agriculture Insurance and Risk Professional.

Thank you to my publisher Taylor & Francis for the opportunity and their assistance.

Finally, thank you to my partner Cheryl Lacey for her continued support.

Other Works by Clifton Warren

Financial Services Sales Handbook
Cross-Selling Financial Services
Rain Maker Pro
99 Frequently Asked Questions about Marketing and Selling Financial Services
Podcast: Clifton's Top Producer
Newsletter: Clifton's Top Producer
Blog: Clifton's Sales Insights

Introduction

The first professional salesman I ever met was Bill Blankenship, a recruiter for the US Navy. I went to the Navy recruiting center across the street from my high school to learn about joining the Navy. Bill immediately sold me; as I was only 17, I needed the permission of my mother. Bill came to my home, met my mother and other family members, and explained why joining the Navy was a good idea, especially for a young man just finishing high school. He sold my mother on the idea.

That sparked my interest in selling. I landed my first sales job in the financial services industry in California. I didn't get off to such a great start, but I still had the passion for selling.

Since then, I have lived and traveled to several continents working as a sales professional, and as a sales leader working in multinational companies. I've led and developed sales teams and along the way met hundreds of top professionals and leaders who shared their challenges, issues, and successes.

I decided to launch my own consulting practice. I've had the opportunity to coach and train hundreds of professionals, teaching them how to build a great career and lifestyle through selling.

Why I wrote this book

Research shows that one in nine people in the United States directly works in sales. A similar ratio applies to countries like Australia and New Zealand and if you consider business owners, self-employed professionals, and partners in service firms across law, accounting, and consulting, that number is even greater. Our economy more than ever relies on service industries and the selling of intangibles.

Business to business selling can appear mysterious, especially to those who are new to selling.

DOI: 10.4324/9781003364580-1

I wrote this book to help demystify sales, to make selling skills and techniques accessible to those who need to acquire them to help grow their business.

This book is written for four types of professionals:

1 Business to business sales professionals who sell services such as banking insurance finance and other intangibles.
2 Self-employed business owners including lawyers, accountants, engineers, partners, and service companies that must sell for a living.
3 Experienced sales professionals who need to update or refresh their skills.
4 Professionals in other areas who are making the transition into selling.

How this book is written

This book is divided into 26 short chapters, one letter for each of the alphabet. The book contains lessons to help readers navigate the selling of complex than intangible solutions. Each chapter covers an important concept that every sales professional should be familiar with. It also includes takeaways action list, so this can be used both as a workbook and a study guide.

By reading each section and applying the steps mentioned in each chapter, you will substantially improve your sales performance.

My goal is to help you develop your capabilities to make big things happen in your business. I hope this book will help you along that journey.

Chapter 1

A – Accountability

Breaking through your natural ceiling

What is accountability?

Accountability provides an outside perspective by stripping away excuses so that you can see yourself in an honest and unblinking manner.

Accountability is the starting point for high sales achievement. It's a powerful tool to help you achieve big sales goals and develop good sales habits and activities to build a great sales career and lifestyle. Accountability begins by taking ownership of your outcomes and holding only yourself responsible for your results.

Why is accountability important?

To achieve your objectives, you should focus on implementing your sales plans, setting activity goals in prospecting, and preparing presentations. You must try to balance the demands of existing clients' relationships with getting new business.

The next thing you know you've to hit a ceiling or plateau. When this happens, people will often say, "I'm doing the best, and this is the best I can do."

At some point, everyone hits a natural achievement ceiling – similarly to a baseball player hitting a batting slump or NBA basketball star Steph Curry experiencing a shooting slump. Regardless of whether you run your own business or are part of a larger organization, if you have a responsibility for generating new business, you will hit a ceiling.

Accountability is the key to breaking through the achieving ceiling and exceeding new heights. This requires focusing on your key result areas and maintaining that focus over the short and long terms.

How does accountability work?

Accountability is a process that you do with someone else. You need someone on a weekly, monthly, and quarterly basis to hold you accountable

DOI: 10.4324/9781003364580-2

for your results. Some professionals are more disciplined than others. Some professionals might have greater focus, but it's difficult to hold yourself accountable continually.

Effective accountability is about being careful about what you focus on and then helping you maintain that focus at a high level.

Sales accountability requires you to take individual ownership of your responsibilities for production and the key result areas of your role. It helps shape and reshape your focus on the activities you need for success.

You get the best accountability through a relationship that follows a process to help you refocus regularly. This could be your sales leader, a coach, a mastermind group, a colleague, or any individual who you will meet with on a scheduled basis to review your goals and results.

Be upfront and forthcoming about your sales performance and be willing to discuss your shortcomings. Share your goals and deal with your actions and results, don't hide.

What is the accountability loop?

Set your objectives and goals: You must know your numbers, the targets you want to achieve. Your goals also provide the best potential areas for growth, ensuring that you do not overlook any opportunities. You should include activity and results goals.

Do the activities: The day-to-day activities to achieve your objectives, including lead generation, prospecting, and referrals.

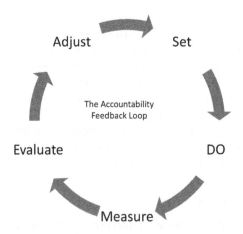

Figure 1.1 The five-step accountability process.

Measure your results: Tracking your numbers and results – for example, news leads, meetings, number of presentations, new clients, and referrals.
Evaluate your process: To determine what is working well.
Adjust: Your activities and goals as necessary to stay on track.

The accountability feedback loop is an empowering process for continual focus and refocus on developing the right skills and traits for success (Figure 1.1).

Why is self-accountability difficult?

Accountability provides feedback so that you can see yourself in an honest and unblinking manner. It's tough to face the reality of your own behavior and on level of effort every day, and taking complete ownership of your outcomes by holding only you're self-responsible for them is the most powerful thing you can do to drive sales success.

It's far too easy to get distracted and lose focus (see Chapter 6); for example, in trying to balance client demands against new business, your objectives can become off track. You start with an aim of spending 40% of your time on new business activities to achieve growth. However, before you know it, you're spending 80% or more of your time servicing existing clients' needs instead of getting new ones.

Getting focus is easy, but keeping it over time is not. And to be your best, you must focus on your goals and objectives daily. This can feel like a routine, particularly when you're trying to balance other demands of your business, and that leads to boredom. When boredom sets in, your attention drifts, the mind wanders, and before you know it, you have fallen to the service trap. Having an outside perspective strips away the excuses.

You don't see this right away because you are in the middle of action. You have good intentions of getting back on track but never seem to. Following the accountability loop with a coach or manager, this shift is detected early and corrective action is taken to get you back on track.

Accountability keeps you on track with a long-term focus on the smallest number of activities that will generate results. For example, following the 80/20 rule (20% of your activities will generate 80% of your results) ensures that you are focusing on those activities and results and on your time to achieve your results. You maintain that balance and focus with feedback. That is why accountability is tough to apply on your own.

Accountability is a big part of the success of the multibillion-dollar weight loss industry with companies such Weight Watchers. The programs work similarly. You set your goals in this case, your target ideal weight, you do the activity of your meals and exercise; you have your personal coaching with someone else outside to help you monitor your progress and give you feedback. This same process applies to sales accountability.

Accountability is the single most important difference between an average and a top-producing professional who seeks teachers and coaches and engages in supervised training, whereas the average performers rarely engage in similar activities. Everyone has habits and behaviors and biases and skills that at some point can create a ceiling.

Nearly all champions and high achievers such as LeBron James, Tiger Woods, Naomi Osaka, and Lauren Jackson have coaches to provide accountability to help keep themselves on track and achieve their huge goals. It also works for athletes, businesspeople, and top sales professionals.

How do you implement an accountability process?

Having an outside perspective helps strip away the excuses so that you can see yourself in an honest and unblinking manner. Keep track and feed it back. I recommend following a five-step accountability process:

1 Select a person – this could be a coach, mentor, peer, or mastermind group.
2 Meet on a regularly scheduled basis to review your goals and results.
3 Bring along and share your goals, business plan, and activities.
4 Summarize the results you've achieved to date.
5 Determine the frequency. Weekly or bi-weekly schedule is a good starting point. I know some top professionals who have daily meetings (phone, virtually, or in person) with their coach or consultant.

Just do it! Adjust the process to fit your needs and circumstance.

Top performer perspective

Simon Swanston, Managing Director, ClearView

What does ClearView do?

ClearView is an ASX-listed Australian financial services group specializing in life insurance, superannuation, and wealth management advice.

How many people do you have?

300

How do you create a culture of accountability across your business?

We have six key inputs: integrity, understanding, knowledge, capacity, knowledge, and experience. We regularly meet and monitor the team around these six areas to ensure that we stay on track to achieve our objectives.

Key takeaways

- Accountability provides an outside perspective by stripping away excuses so that you can see yourself in an honest and unblinking manner.
- Accountability is the starting point for high sales achievement. It's a powerful tool to help you achieve big sales goals and develop good sales habit.
- Accountability is the key to breaking through the achieving ceiling and exceeding new heights. This requires focusing on your key result areas and maintaining that focus over the short and long terms.
- Accountability keeps you on track with a long-term focus on the smallest number of activities that will generate the results.
- Accountability is the single most important difference between an average and a top-producing professional who seeks teachers and coaches and engages in supervised training.

Chapter 2

B – Beliefs

Making the first sale to yourself

What is a belief?

Belief is an attitude or firmly held opinion that something is the case or that some proposition is true.

There is a story of three blind men who lived in a land where an elephant was the principal beast of burden. These men blind from birth had never seen an elephant. One day they fell into discussing what an elephant might be like. As they talked, they decided to satisfy their curiosity by going out to the side of the highway until they found an elephant.

By chance, one blind man placed his hand on the elephant's great massive side. The second person reached out and touched the elephant's trunk, and the third person held in his hand the elephant's tail. Then they turned and retraced their steps. As they walked, the first blind man said, "I found to much surprise that an elephant is like a great smooth wall." Disagreeing, the second said, "No, you're wrong. An elephant is like a trunk of a tree." "No," said the third, "You're both wrong. I found the elephant is like a piece of rope." Each of these men had a limited concept of an elephant. If they had been able to hold in their hand an accurately carved miniature of an elephant and explore its shape with their fingertips, then it would have helped them to develop a broader understanding of the appearance of an elephant.

In much the same way, to one individual, your service offering is like a great wall; to another, it's like a tree trunk; and to a third one, it is but a piece of rope. However, as a professional dedicated to serving their clients, the entire picture is clear – you see all the broad avenues and value that your offering delivers.

Why are beliefs important?

Professionals will seldom find it necessary to put their concepts of their offerings into words, but the mere possession of a broader understanding

DOI: 10.4324/9781003364580-3

of your value will increase your ability to help prospect and clients understand and appreciate it.

The first sale is always to yourself. This often can be the toughest sale to make because of insecurity and fear. Belief in your products and services and belief in yourself are interchangeable. It is impossible to have a firm belief in yourself if you really don't respect the value of what you sell; it takes a strong confidence in your offering to become excited about it and when you're excited others will get excited; you relay a powerful message to your client that you have their best interests at heart.

How do you develop a belief in your offering?

It begins with preparation, pulling your services apart, and putting it back together again using various scenarios and internal role-plays, situations, and applications to prospective clients' situations. This helps you develop the confidence to prospect, obtain meetings, and conversatiuons to help prospective clients.

A strong belief in your offering is an important part of building your personal brand (see Chapter 25) and prevent you from being seen as a commodity.

You must do your homework to fully understand the value (Chapter 21) of your offering. A financial advisor needs to understand various ways of estate planning, budgeting, insurance, and taxation. Architects must understand building design, planning regulations, and project management.

When you do your homework, you will become fully prepared when you are in the moment with a prospect.

One of the most prolific salespeople of all time was Ben Feldman, in 1979 he sold more life insurance than anyone else in history. When asked about how he could sell such an intangible product as life insurance, he responded, "I do not sell life insurance, I sell money. I sell dollars for pennies apiece. My dollars cost 3 cents per dollar per year." Ben learned early in his career that you must know what you are doing. Ben would spend hours with a rate book until he knew it inside and out, upside down. He knew the rate book was just mechanics: 2 plus 2 makes 4. He had to understand it by making it simple. He could then confidently speak with a prospect.

By doing your homework of pulling your offering apart and reassembling it you will understand the full value of how it works and benefits a client, and this in turn builds your belief, which becomes contagious.

What are misbeliefs?

The first sale starts with you, just as enthusiasm is contagious, so true is the opposite doubt. A professional who lacks confidence in their offering can easily transmit those feelings to a perceptive client who then becomes uncertain.

Top performers have firm beliefs about their values and thinking. Here are seven misbeliefs that often hold back promising sales careers:

1 I'm not a natural-born salesperson.
2 I can't find the time for selling.
3 I don't have the right knowledge.
4 My clients don't want to deal with a salesperson.
5 I'm not an extrovert.
6 I'm an introvert.
7 I don't know enough people.

When I visit my hi-fi store to check out the latest product releases of speakers, amplifiers, and turntables, it's clear when I speak with the staff that they know what they're talking about. They regularly take equipment home to try it out themselves. They use it daily and they speak with belief and conviction about their offering and service.

The first sale you make to yourself, however, it can be the hardest because of your insecurity, fears, and other self-limiting beliefs.

How do you develop the right mindset?

Top professionals ask themselves if I were the client, would I buy this over a competitor?

This is an excellent test of your belief in your offering by asking, "would you own it yourself?"

People buy what they want from people they like, and since you cannot force someone to buy it, it is up to you to make your ideas attractive so that a prospect will want to do business with you.

When you develop a powerful belief in your offering, you develop the right mindset; you feel you have an obligation to call on prospective clients as you know your offering improves and will improve theirs.

What is a sales philosophy?

Whether you realize it, you already have a sales philosophy determined by your belief and attitude toward selling. Top professionals combine their selling ability with their convictions and beliefs. This becomes a winning combination a unique position over your competitors.

Questions to ask include the following:

- How strongly do you believe in your offering?
- Do you walk the talk?
- Do you view what you do and sell as a higher calling that requires superb skill or knowledge and integrity?

Examples of people with great conviction and philosophy include Abraham Lincoln, Winston Churchill, Ronald Reagan, and Steve Jobs. They used a combination of sales ability and conviction to get their message and ideas across, that is, the ability to persuade.

Top performer perspective

Robert B. Kelly, CEO, Steadfast Group Ltd

What does Steadfast do?

Steadfast Group is the largest general insurance broker network and the largest group of insurance underwriting agencies in Australasia, with growing operations in Asia and Europe.

Steadfast Group has three business units primarily focused on the intermediated general insurance market.

How large is Steadfast today?

It has 427 network brokerages and 28 underwriting agencies, generating $13 billion in total billings.

Have your beliefs and attitudes changed with increased compliance and government regulation?

No, not at all. I've always believed that advice, ethical behavior, and reliability are the sustainable traits in any business. Somebody who has to act in the utmost good faith and the best for their clients is going to be sustainable and endure over a long period of time.

I was fortunate enough to recognize that instead of compliance ruining the industry, it was going to turn it into a quasi-profession.

Key takeaways

- Professionals will seldom find it necessary to put their concepts of their offerings into words, but the mere possession of a broader understanding of your value will increase your ability to help prospect and clients understand and appreciate it.
- The first sale is always to yourself. This often can be the toughest sale to make because of insecurity and fear.
- It begins with preparation, pulling your services apart, and putting it back together again using various scenarios and internal role-plays, situations, and applications to prospective clients' situations.
- When you do your homework, you will become fully prepared when you are with a prospect.
- Top professionals combine their selling ability with their convictions and beliefs. A winning combination gives you a unique position over your competitors.

Chapter 3

C – Client centered

Maximizing your vital few

What is client centered?

A client-centered approach is about developing superior and continuing relationships with your desirable clients. After you establish this relationship, your primary task is to sense, serve, sell, and satisfy the hot-button needs and expectations of everyone involved in the recommendation of the services and solutions that you offer.

Being client-centered is about creating a proactive service model for your very best clients to maximize their lifetime value. Reserve this for the top 20% of your clients that generate up to 80% of your revenues and for those with the highest potential for future growth.

A client-centered approach makes it easier for leveraging your existing client relationships. It's a market-driven approach that puts the client in center of your marketing activities and maximizes key relationships with key players. Marketing approaches that are not client focused as are hard sell and reactive.

There are seven advantages of a client-centered approach:

1 Generates profitable growth from existing clients
2 Makes easier to expand services to existing clients
3 Improves retention of your desirable clients
4 Helps fill your sales pipeline with high potential prospects
5 Capitalizes on the potential of your business, particularly if you're focusing on certain markets
6 Helps you package your expertise effectively
7 Helps you better manage your image within your clients and niche markets

A client-centered approach allows you to work from your comfort zone. This makes marketing and selling easier, which means that it's more likely to get done.

DOI: 10.4324/9781003364580-4

What is the vital few concept?

The "law of the vital few" or "the Pareto principle" is named after Italian sociologist and economist Vilfredo Pareto, who observed in the early 20th century that 80% of the land in Italy was owned by 20% of the population. The 80–20 rule is dominant in various fields, like business.

The Pareto principle states that for many outcomes, roughly 80% of consequences come from 20% of causes (the "vital few"). This law applies to your clients. Twenty percent of your clients will generate 80% of revenues.

A common mistake of many professionals is treating every client equally. A client that pays very little receives "A" class service at the expense of a top client. Bigger clients generate more revenue and take up less time. Smaller transactional clients can chew up a large amount of your time for a small return.

This is the reason you should segment your clients to identify the top 20%. This also includes existing clients with the potential to become top 20% clients and delegate the rest. If you are an independant professional, have an assistant handle the smaller transaction-type clients, to avoid the service trap.

How do you segment clients?

Focus on your time and effort on your top 20% of clients who generate 80% of the revenue and stop providing "A" class service to "C" class clients. I recommend the ABC method to segment your clients by revenue:

- Category A: the top 5%
- Category B: the next 15%
- Category C: the bottom 80%

This makes it easy to package and deliver service in a similar way an airline offers first class, business, and economy with different levels of services and distinctions. You should focus 80% of your time proactively managing your categories "A" and "B" clients' relationships, cross-selling, and getting referrals.

Your client-centered program puts the client in the center of your marketing. Your top clients receive the full benefits of your client-centered program – making it easier to leverage your client relationships for new ones and better manage your time (Chapter 20).

Avoid your service being viewed as a commodity from a buyer's perspective:

- The recipient always defines value, not the provider.
- Clients don't purchase your service offering, they are buying your promise to work with them to create a favourable result.

- Services really bought in the client's gut. They justify their decision by using a proposal, which testimonial, you know, to support their decision.
- Clients know what they want, but not always know what they need.

Your role as a professional is to educate your clients and prospects on your value offerings.

I visited my local shoe store where I've been a regular customer for several years to purchase a new pair of shoes that I'd seen in the window. I knew what I wanted. The owner took the time to ask me several questions about the reason I wanted to purchase the shoes. Were they for business or pleasure? What type of clothes would I be wearing? I ended with something quite different that better matched my needs in both style and comfort, and I was happy to pay a little extra. I'm a happy and loyal customer. The owner and his staff are customer centric, and they generate 80% of their business from repeat customers and referrals, they don't advertise.

What is client lifetime value?

Client lifetime value is the total amount of revenue we expect a client to generate during the lifetime of the average relationship. For example, if an average relationship generates $5,000 per year annually and they remains with you for ten years, their lifetime value is $50,000.

A neglected aspect of selling is failing to maximize the potential locked up in the client base – not seeking to increase sales from existing clients. It's accepted that it costs between five and seven times as much to get a client as to keep one (Chapter 17).

A client-centered program will allow you to proactively enhance your client relationship and maximize the long-term value of your very best clients by having a focused process that is your proprietary process for your business that only you can deliver, which is tailor-made for each client.

"Client centered" is a mindset and approach. It's a way of doing business that makes you distinct from your competitors. It's something that your clients can only get from doing business with you.

Client-centered approach maximizes the long-term value and profits from existing clients:

- You don't just have a client transaction, you have a relationship.
- Enables you to better allocate your resources.
- Helps identify prospective clients within your portfolio that have the potential to become "A" or "B" level clients.
- Provides a way to nurture and grow with your smaller clients.

Your client-centered model is the ideal platform for training and developing your staff by having a common and consistent process that's followed by everyone in the business.

Continuation is your key to creating a point of difference, having a unique competitive advantage maximizing the long-term value of your desired clients by:

- Increasing the number of clients
- Increasing the average size of accounts
- Increasing the frequency, that is, how many times a client does business with you

Your client-centered approach puts you in control of these factors and just a 10% increase in any of these areas can lead to tremendous revenue growth.

Top performer perspective

Bernie McIntosh, Managing Director, Victoria Mortgage Group

What does Victoria Mortgage Group do?

Victorian Mortgage Group is a family-owned and managed business. We provide flexible lending solutions for finance broker to assist their clients with home loans, debt consolidation, and small business lending.

How long have you been operating?

We were founded in 1946 at a different time but evolved into Victoria Mortgage Group. We begin by assisting return servicemen into the housing market. There was a government lending program, and we were called in to help manage that lending program.

How do you deliver client-focused services?

Some brokers need assistance with the types of loans we offer. When they come across an opportunity, we might try to approach a bank to arrange funding. When the bank declines the deal, we offer a friendly helping hand and try and work alongside them to help their clients find the right type of loan.

Key takeaways

- A client-centered approach is about developing superior and continuing relationships with your desirable clients.
- Being client-centered is about creating a proactive service model for your very best clients to maximize their lifetime value.
- It's a market-driven approach that puts the client at the center of your marketing activities and maximizes relationships with key players.
- A common mistake of many professionals is treating every client equally.
- Your client-centered model is the ideal platform for training and developing your staff members across your business by having a common and consistent process that's being followed by everyone in the business.

Chapter 4

D – Discipline

Maximizing your strengths

What is self-discipline?

Self-discipline refers to achieving your desirable outcomes. For example, getting up early to maintain your fitness. When you proactively contact and follow up prospective clients, is self-discipline by performing repeated positive actions of consistency. Self-discipline is also persistence. It's a measure of your beliefs in your service offerings.

Self-discipline is the key to sales mastery and the more capable you are at disciplining yourself to do what you have done regardless of whether you feel like it or not, the more powerful you'll feel, the better results you will produce.

Top professionals don't wait for things to deteriorate so drastically that someone else must impose discipline. Instead, they take charge by ensuring they are doing the right things at the right time and using accountability (Chapter 1) to help stay on track and focused.

Why is discipline important?

The Life Insurance Marketing and Research Association conducted research by contacting over 500 individuals who had failed as agents before they had been in the business for 18 months. These individuals appeared to be qualified to sell insurance and, on paper, looked like they would succeed. The researcher asked: "What did you find most difficult about selling life insurance?" The answer that was mentioned three times more than any other was the discipline of prospecting, finding people to market and sell to.

Jim Ron says, "The key to getting all you want is discipline, and the most valuable form of discipline is the one you impose upon yourself." Success is a long game, not the quick game of instant gratification.

I've always been a self-starter willing to learn more.

(Kylie Stephens, Broker)

DOI: 10.4324/9781003364580-5

Former life insurance sales professional and author Frank Bettger once said that few men in selling fail because they can't sell, they fail because they lack self-discipline and direction.

What is the law of familiarity?

Discipline also falls into the category of the law of familiarity. Everything affects everything else if you neglect self-discipline and there'll be a price to pay. For example, if you're not doing enough prospecting, you will not have enough people to call upon. When you don't have enough people to call upon, you have no one to present your offering, which will ultimately lead to poor sales results. If you don't have the discipline to follow through on your client-focused model, retention will suffer as clients leave for elsewhere, affecting the profitability of your business.

Self-discipline is the stability of controlling yourself and to make yourself work hard and behave particularly with no one else to tell you, you know what to do. It is a learned behavior. The first step to self-discipline is building a pyramid of priorities. First things first and to make every minute count, it becomes a part of clearly defining your goals. Knowing what you stand for and where you are going and leveraging your coaches, advisors, and mentors by using your accountability (see Chapter 1) help you stay focused and stay on track.

What is a pyramid of priorities?

Selling is a skill that requires you to work on daily, and diligently, in the areas associated with your goals, including prospecting, getting meetings, qualifying prospects, presenting your offerings, handling objections, following up, and asking for referrals.

We need to have a bridge a clear pathway with time-bound steps you know you must take. Self-discipline, is the bridge between your goals and your desired accomplishments to help you to develop and control your habits and the choices you make.

I first discovered self-discipline when I was 17 years old in the US Navy. Bootcamp is the starting point for everyone. Nine weeks of basic training (now ten weeks) comprising physical conditioning, learning customs, hands-on training, weapons training, and firefighting. This process can take a 17-year-old kid and turn them into a sailor in just a few short weeks. The Navy provided the program, but it takes self-discipline to master and apply it during your career.

What is the endless chain concept?

In building your pyramid of priorities, focus on doing the first things first by identifying your big rocks.

Jerry Seinfeld, who is a very successful comedian, learned very early on about the discipline of success. Jokes are a comedian's tool of trade; they need an ample supply of fresh jokes. Jerry Seinfeld understood this and disciplined himself. He set up a big wall calendar in his office, and each day he wrote a new joke he would put an X through that day. Over a period, he saw a lot of red Xs, meaning that he worked that day to create a new joke. Thirty days equaled 30 jokes. Once he gained the habit, he did not want to break the chain. He turned his joke writing discipline into a game, continually creating new material.

The endless chain concept applies to selling. For example, when you set a prospecting goal of generating two new leads per day, put an X on your calendar that day. And don't break that chain. That's putting your big rock first to ensure you have a steady stream of prospective clients to keep your sales pipeline overflowing with opportunities.

Sometimes things will not work out the way we want them to. As the saying goes, some days it's going to rain on your parade. You take two steps forward and one step back. Life is like that. We make a little progress here and a little progress there. We regress, but we continue to advance with self-discipline.

How do I implement self-discipline?

A good starting point is that focus on the essentials:

- Put prospecting at the top.
- Getting your prospecting done early builds momentum for the rest of your day.
- Review your goals and break your plans in small doable steps instead of trying to change everything at once.
- Do micro actions each day to help propel you toward your goals.
- Use accountability to help you stay focused and stay on track.

Top performer perspective

Richard Crawford, CEO, Community Broker Network

What is the history of CBN?

The Community Broker Network (CBN) was formed following the acquisition of two General Insurance Broker groups.

How large is CBN?

We have over 900 authorized advisors and staff. $900 million turnover. We consider ourselves a community rather than a more traditional organization. At the center of the community is my team, which kind of helps the community to organize itself.

How do you approach discipline?

I think at a CEO and individual level, there's a whole lot of responsibility about how I show up because it's an absolute truth that ultimately how I show up has at least 50% of the impact on our team. Daily I spend quite a lot of time in planning, journaling, thinking, doing some reading, getting some positive inspiration about what business leaders are thinking and doing, and also what personal leaders are thinking and doing.

I start each day with that with my team. I always create a listening space for them, and I coach and mentor them and encourage them to tell me what's working as well as what's not.

From my time in field experience

Self-discipline is one of the most important traits you can develop as a sales professional along with persistence. Selling is a process of two steps forward and one step back at times. You make progress then regress; clients sometimes cancel or fail to show up for appointments. Sometimes you receive several "No's" before getting a "Yes." Regardless of the outcome focus on your activity, results will take care of themselves. The law of averages will work in your favor, but you need to apply discipline.

Know your numbers and follow your plan. The discipline of spending 30 minutes per day contacting prospects, over the course of a month that's 10 hours marketing, a small portion of time will provide a great return in new clients and growth.

Key takeaways

- Self-discipline is persistence. It's a measure of your beliefs in your service offerings.
- Self-discipline is the key to sales mastery and the more capable you are at disciplining yourself to do what you have done regardless of you feel like it or not, the more powerful you'll feel, and the better results you will produce.
- Few people in selling fail because they can't sell, they fail because they lack self-discipline and direction.

- We need to have a bridge also for ourselves, a clear pathway with time-bound steps you know you must take, and self-discipline is a bridge between your goals and your desired accomplishments.
- The discipline of prospecting should be at the top of your list.
- Do micro actions each day to help propel you toward your goals.
- Use accountability to help you stay focused and stay on track.

Chapter 5

E – End results

Knowing what you want

At the end of the day, you can't control the results; you can only control your effort level and focus.

(Ben Zobrist)

What is begging with the end in mind?

Begging with the end in mind means to think about how you would like something to turn out before you get started. Top professionals begin with their end results and work backward. They are clear about their objectives and the activities for their clients and the best route to get there. They understand that achievement is first created in the mind, followed by the activity.

PK is a professional at an architectural firm that specializes in designing homes for affluent buyers and investors. She joined her firm as an architect. She recognized early in her career that the fastest way to get promoted and eventually become a partner was to learn how to sell and bring in additional work instead of waiting for work to be handed to her by the firms' founders.

Less than three years in the business, she is making the founders and established professionals in her firm to sit up and take notice. She has built a clientele that will continue to grow, and she will grow with them. How did PK make it where others had missed?

She takes a long-term view of her business and understands her firms' objectives and the role she plays, aligning her personal growth objectives and knowing what's needed to achieve their objectives. She has clarity on her direction and destination. She focused on the proactive things to make that happen.

DOI: 10.4324/9781003364580-6

What is an ideal client?

A financial services firm once approached me for help with getting new clients. When I asked for a description of their ideal client, the reply was "Everyone needs our services." This helped explain why this firm was struggling to grow. They were trying to be all things to all people and failing.

Knowing your ideal client begins with fully understanding your value offering and then defining the types of businesses who that would benefit from your value offering. Targeting is not simply a numbers game. Top performers handpick their markets, individuals, and organizations to maximize their time, energy, and return on investment.

For many professionals business development is one of several hats you must wear. When you focus your limited time on business development, you don't have the time to waste on nonproductive activities.

How do you identify your ideal client?

Here are seven ways to identify your ideal client:

1 Your current client base
2 Their current habits
3 Identify their goals
4 Determine how they buy
5 Your dream list
6 What they need
7 Identify their fears

Your current client base

Segment your clients (see Chapter 3) into A, B, and C categories. Categories A and B should follow the 80/20 rule. They will be the top 20% generating up to 80% of your revenues. Review their industry, location, and reasons as to why you enjoy working with them. Identify who makes the buying decision. Ask your clients why they like to do business with you.

What are their habits?

Research what they read, membership associations, and where they hang out. What are the triggers for using your offering. Connect on LinkedIn and other social media platforms to identify trends.

What are their goals?

Research your top clients' industry and markets. Review their top competitors and what they are doing. Are they leaders or followers? Ask your best clients for help.

How do they buy?

Identify who has the buying authority and if they purchase directly for the provider or if there is a tender process. How often do they purchase?

Create a dream list

Review your existing client base and develop a list of your existing clients' competitors. Purchase a list of similar companies. Leverage the industry associations of your top clients many of these produce membership list.

Identify needs

Look for trends, new regulations, and compliance requirements that may signal a need for your services. Interview the executives of trade associations for their views on industry trends.

Identify fears

People often make decisions for two reasons: either they have a need that they would like to fulfill or they have a problem that they need to solve. Research the problems that your potential clients are facing and offer them a solution to help bridge the gap. Review the reason why your existing clients use your offering. This will provide clues for their competitors who might be facing similar issues.
Define the ideal clients for your business by asking the following questions:

- What opportunities exist in the selected markets?
- What is the best way to reach this market?
- What will be your approach?
- What is the ideal number of client profiles?

You can and often should have more than one ideal client profile. For an individual professional, I recommend 1–3 and for a business 5–7. Clearly defining your ideal clients helps you to filter down the universe, provide the focus and discipline, then use accountability to stay focused and on track with your goals and activities to translate your sales plans into reality.

What is a whole client view?

Building superior relationships with your clients beyond just the transaction including:

- Having 100% full-time clients. They're doing all their business with you and not with your competitor.
- Following an effective client-focused model to exceed their expectations.
- Focusing on relationship building and a strong partnership.

Eight categories of questions to ask your clients:

Professional background

- How long have you owned or been with your company?
- Describe your background – what did you do before you started, bought, or came into this business?
- What are your goals?

Business profile

- Describe what your business does completely. Products and services, you sell and how you sell them? Whom do you sell to by industry?
- Specific niche?
- Who has the highest propensity of buying from you?

Clients or customers

- How many active customers do you have?
- How many "dream" clients are there (that 20% that would drive 80% of your sales)?
- What is your biggest and best source of new business?

Sales force

- Do you have inside sales – people?
- Describe your sales team.
- What are their strengths and weaknesses and where they're utilized?

Marketing

- What is your target market and how did you arrive at it?

- What is your market potential (universe)? What is your current share of that market?
- Describe the company's marketing philosophy.

Strategic partners

- What strategic alliances do you currently have?
- Who are your suppliers or other providers of products or services that benefit massively when you are successful?
- What is your unique selling proposition?

Competitors

- Describe all you know about your competitors.
- Where are your top three competitors located?
- What do they do best?

The better you know your clients, the more ways you can add value. The more ways you can help them, the more effective results you'll achieve.

By starting with your end results and working backward, you can create an effective plan to attract, retain, and develop great clients. Ultimately, it's about the value you're delivering that solves a client's problem and/or improves their condition.

You must balance client and business demands. This includes servicing existing clients and business development. With regard to all your sales activities you need to be proactive in your service delivery and have the discipline and accountability (Chapter 1) to achieve it.

Top performer perspective

Joe Arena, CEO, Procurement Australia

What does Procurement Australia do?

We work in close partnership with long-standing and emerging suppliers and members to find and deliver the most innovative and sustainable supply chain solutions. Throughout our long history, we've continued to evolve and grow as a business in order to best support our members' procurement goals, no matter their size or industry.

What is the size of your team?

We have 20 staff in Victoria and about 15 in New South Wales and about 5 contractors. In addition, we have representation in Queensland and South Australia.

How do you focus on end results with your clients?

Our focus is to always deliver a 10/10 level of customer service for all our members. The Procurement Australia team has decades of experience across all our business areas, making us one of the most skilled procurement teams in Australia. Our goal is to ensure that every member gets what they need the first time around.

My time in the field

Whatever your goal is, always work backward to create bite-size chunks, and you can easily get your hands around. Use self-discipline (Chapter 4) to set a realistic schedule you can follow each day. Constantly expand your end results to stretch yourself and expand your comfort zone.

Key takeaways

- Top professionals begin with their end results and work backward.
- Knowing your ideal client begins with fully understanding your value offering and then defining the individual or organization that would best benefit from your value offering.
- There are seven ways to identify your ideal client.
- You need to balance your client and business demands. This includes servicing existing clients and business development.
- The better you know your clients, the more ways you can add value. The more ways can help them, the more effective results you'll achieve.

Chapter 6

F – Focus

Finding your doughnut

What is a personal doughnut?

Charles Handy coined the phrase the "doughnut principle," which is a concept of balancing between what we must do and what we could do. Dunkin sells classic American-style doughnuts which have a hole in the middle. The heart of the doughnut contains all the things which must be done in a job or role if you are not to fail. They often list these in a job description or duties (Figure 6.1).

The core is, however, not the whole doughnut. Similarly, your job description is not your complete job. Boredom is a big problem in the workforce today, including sales. It's not just the routine, which average professionals blame, that causes the boredom, it's the endlessness of what they are doing. They just never seem to arrive at any destination – they lack focus and never seem to get anywhere simply because they don't have a destination.

Like Alice in Wonderland, they never learned the process of goal setting, shifting through choices, and focusing. They may have heard or read about it but cannot assimilate the meaning of their own career. They are only focusing on the core of the doughnut that is filled with chores.

Top professionals go beyond their core to gain, keep, and develop clients, creating a well-developed doughnut to stimulate our thinking about the balance between commitment and flexibility.

Early in my career in financial services, I was promoted to branch manager of an insurance company. Everyone knew my predecessor in the industry and the local market. I came in as an outsider with few contacts and relationships. I was following my job description, checking off items, and doing things so that I would not fail. Within six months I had lost 25% of my clients, and at the current rate I was going to be out of the job in about 12 months.

I went to my boss complaining; he reminded me that my job was to sell, and I'm here for my capabilities. From that point on, I only used my job description as a guide, and I threw out the old playbook and developed a

DOI: 10.4324/9781003364580-7

Figure 6.1 Your doughnut.

prospecting and lead generation approach that allowed me to work from my comfort zone and leverage my strengths.

Within six months, I had stabilized the losses and within 12 months I turned the whole situation around. I built doughnut that went beyond the core of my job descriptions. My doughnut became my focus that helped me to develop a terrific career.

What are models?

A sales model is a core strategy and process for doing business. Everyone has a model. The difference between top and average professionals is that top professionals purposely choose big models in the key areas that matter. The right model helps you focus your efforts on the trivial few – the top 20% of activities that generated 80% of results.

It's easy to become distracted by many things that are competing for your attention. Maintaining focus is the key to long-term success. Following the right model can have huge rewards.

There are four types of models (see Figure 6.2).

Sales model

Sales model describes the relationship between your activities and the specific outcome they produce. Everyone has a sale as a model. The question is, "do you understand the one you have and is it helping you to achieve your objectives and produce the desired results?"

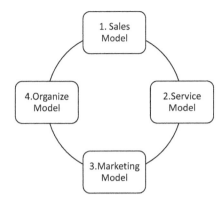

Figure 6.2 **Focus models.**

A sales model includes three focusing activities:

1 Focusing on the numbers you must hit – your overall sales and/or growth goals.
2 Focusing on the number of appointments – meetings with prospective clients.
3 Focusing on the conversion rates and meeting clients.

Service model

Service model is at the heart of your client-centered approach (see Chapter 3) for proactively managing your existing key client relationships (trivial few) with top 20% and existing "C" clients with long-term future growth potential.

Key areas of your service model include the following:

1 A formal process for proactively managing top 20% of client relationships
2 Retention strategies for your top 20% of clients
3 Leveraging top client relationships for referrals

Marketing model

Your marketing model is just as important as your sales model. Once you know the number of appointments you must have, you have to generate the leads necessary to generate those appointments. Leads are the fuel to your planning engine and you can never have enough good leads.

Three key areas of your marketing model include:

1 Your chosen markets and prospects
2 Database of suspects and prospective clients
3 Systematically marketing to your database to generate new leads

Organization model

When you've hit that ceiling, you are getting all the results you can get and can't go any further, you need to look for help. This help should come in the form of talent.

Three key areas of your organization model include:

1 Acknowledging that you need help and seeking out the right kind of help
2 Finding talent to leverage your business
3 Training your team to teach them how to do their job well and challenge them to grow and learn

Following the right model can have a tremendous impact on your business and deliver some big rewards, both for you personally and professionally.

What is raising the bar?

Raising the bar may be simpler than you think, not just easy, just simpler. It's absolutely possible for everyone to do it with the right focus, but not everyone will. With the right models, you take the guesswork out of your planning, and the key there is to know your numbers, focus on your meetings, and focus on your conversions.

How do you implement these models?

Aim high and focus on the numbers you must hit with the model. Use the worksheet presented in Table 6.1 to fill in your performance numbers and see clearly what is required for you to achieve your sales goals. One area affects the others. Once you get a feel for the way the numbers interact, you take the guesswork out of your planning and are able to set specific goals to obtain the results you need to be a top performer.

Following your sales models will provide focus, beginning with your end results to set specific sales objectives (Chapter 5). You will be better equipped and organized to acquire new business, service existing clients, obtain referrals, and maintain an overflowing sales pipeline of qualified prospective clients. Unfocused professionals waste time in cold calling,

Table 6.1 Sales worksheet

1. Growth Target	%
2. Gross Revenue Necessary	$
3. Less Guaranteed Business	$
4. New Gross Revenue Required	$
5. Average Revenue per Sale	$
6. New Sales Needed (#4 ÷ #5)	
7. Closing Ratio	%
8. Presentations Required (#6 ÷ #7)	
9. Conversion Ratio	%
10. New Meetings Needed (#8 ÷ #9)	

endless meetings with unqualified suspects, and engaging in ad hoc marketing approaches.

Identify the key skills you must learn and upgrade (Chapter 21) to convert leads and suspects into prospects meetings, convert prospects into clients, and leverage clients for referrals, and skills to convert those appointments into sales. If you aim low, you'll achieve low targets. If you aim high, you'll hit your big targets. Top professionals aim high.

Business success or failure doesn't just happen. It's all about the choices, about what you focus on, and how you maintain that focus. Focus on the top 20% big rocks. Write these key goals down them and allocate time to achieve these things in your calendar and create daily plans. Time management will be covered fully in Chapter 20.

Top performer perspective

Allan Manning, Founder and Executive Chairman, LMI Group

When was LMI founded?

February 1999

How did you get started?

I realized that small- and medium-sized businesses needed someone on their side when it came to insurance claims because it was getting harder and harder, and it still gets, it's still difficult to get a valid claim paid. Having someone who knows insurance on the side of the insured seemed like a good idea.

How has your focus expanded?

We now have a law firm, we have a forensic accounting team, we do policy drafting, and we have six online services, policy comparison of business interruption calculator, risk coach, and planning.

My time in the field

Don't wait for your company to hand you an operating manual. Instead, create your own approach and playbook. This will serve you well throughout your career. This is a living document that you keep adding to as you gain more experience. This is a key part of building your personal brand (see Chapter 25).

Key takeaways

- A sales model is a core strategy and process for doing business.
- Top professionals go beyond their core to gain, keep, and develop clients, creating a well-developed doughnut to stimulate our thinking about the balance between commitment and flexibility.
- A sales model is a core strategy and process for doing business. Everyone has a model. The difference between top and average professionals is that top professionals purposely choose big models in the key areas that matter.
- Aim high and focus on the numbers you must hit with the model.
- Business success or failure doesn't just happen. It's all about the choices, about what you focus on and how you maintain that focus.

Chapter 7

G – Goals

Aiming high to hit high targets

What are goals?

Goals are statements of measurable results to be achieved. They become your route marker that provides you with a track to run on. They provide the foundation to help you develop focus (Chapter 6) and provide direction. Without direction, you can wind up in a similar situation like Alice in Wonderland:

Alice:	"Would you tell me, please, which way I ought to go from here?"
The Cheshire Cat:	"That depends a good deal on where you want to get to."
Alice:	"I don't much care where."
The Cheshire Cat:	"Then it doesn't much matter which way you go."
Alice:	"… so long as I get somewhere."
The Cheshire Cat:	"Oh, you're sure to do that, if only you walk long enough."[1]

Why are goals important?

Goal setting in sales is essential. Done properly, goal setting is more than just setting numbers. It should include where you need to focus your efforts and the strategies to help you translate your wishes into reality. They are critical for any professional who has discretion in using resources, including their time, energy, and talent. To get somewhere, you must know three things:

1 Where are you going?
2 How you expect to get there?
3 When you expect to arrive?

For example, if I'm planning a trip to visit my relatives, first, I must decide where I'm going to (e.g., Melbourne, Australia to San Francisco, California);

DOI: 10.4324/9781003364580-8

next, how I expect to get there? (e.g., by plane); and, finally, when I expect to arrive? (e.g., November for thanksgiving). With these details, I can start planning the details and notify the family of my arrival.

Setting goals helps you to know when you win and enables you to determine where to concentrate your efforts. Many professionals work hard at their job, being efficient where the payoff is minimal. Some with the best intentions fall into the service trap of doing the wrong things, on the belief that anything worth doing is worth doing right.

I regularly observed professionals who have transitioned into selling, who are supposed to be generating new revenue, who have in addition to the responsibilities of their individual discipline and expertise of engineering, finance, technology, and so on, and who take pride in having a long to-do list as a source of security. They wind up spending significant effort looking busy with activities at the expense of measurable progress toward what they are ultimately supposed to achieve.

Many are engaged in wrong activities, many of these are not worth doing at all or should be done by someone else. Without clear goals, they lack the direction and focus which has been responsible for stalling many promising sales careers.

How do I establish priorities?

Anytime you elect to pursue one goal instead of another, you have made a priority decision. Some decisions are quite easy. However, when nothing becomes a priority and everything is a priority, it's hard to move.

In other cases, someone else may make a goal decision for you, such as annual sales targets. An easy way to establish priorities is by grouping a list of objectives into the following categories:

- Got-to-do
- Ought-to-do
- Nice-to-do

Got-to-do

These goals are essential. These are the big rocks for your business and career such as achieving financial results, retention of desirable clients, and proactively managing key referral relationships.

Ought-to-do

These are goals where results are likely to provide a significant path forward in the direction you want to go but you have considerable

Table 7.1 Goal priority grouping worksheet

Got-to-do's required	Ought-to-do's significant	Nice-to-do's desired

flexibility: improving visibility within niche market, expanding clientele into new markets, and improving marketing message.

Nice-to-do

These are goals that are desirable but should not get much attention until the go-to-do goals have been completed, for example, expanding territory, updating marketing brochure, and creating a podcast. Use Table 7.1 to layout your goals.

How do you make goals bite size?

You can't swallow a watermelon in one bite. Reducing a goal to a manageable or bite size makes it possible to achieve almost any achievable goal. For example, to achieve a sales target of $750K will require you to achieve growth of 20%.

1 Growth target 20%
2 Gross revenue necessary $750,000
3 Less guaranteed business $600,000
4 Gross revenue needed $150,000
5 Average revenue per sale $15,000
6 Number of new sales needed 10
7 Closing ratio 70%

 8 Presentations needed 14
 9 Conversion ratio 50%
10 First appointments needed 28

There are four categories of sales goals you should set for yourself always:

1 Number of new clients
2 Retention of existing clients
3 Revenue growth
4 Leads

Number of new clients

New clients fuel your growth in revenue and lead generation through referrals and introductions. We can express this as a number, percentage, or both over the previous year. To gain 25 new clients, a 10% increase over the previous year is needed.

Retention

This includes the number of clients and associated revenue. Hundred percent retention of your desirable categories "A" and "B" clients should be the minimum goal.

Revenue

We can express this as a number, percentage, or both over the previous year. To achieve my sales target of $850,000, a 15% growth is needed.

Leads

This is defined as the number of referrals and introductions you have that generate further new business opportunities.

How do I translate goals into action?

Your plans have no value until you translate them into positive action. Reduce your goals to bite-size chunks. Most people set goals that are too broad to be meaningful or manageable or too general to offer a clear sign of what they mean. Goals are statements of measurable results to be achieved. They help you translate your wishes into reality state your goals in terms of measurable results with target dates and cost limitations.

A well-stated goal contains four elements:

1 An action accomplishment verb
2 A single measurable result
3 A target date
4 Cost in terms of money, effort, or both

You want to identify your specific results in a way that you or anyone else can recognize it.

It clearly draws the target so that no question remains about whether or not we have hit the bull's-eye or missed the target altogether.

The model is:

To (action or accomplishment verb) (single measurable results) by (target date) at (cost, hours of effort or both).

Example:

To grow client base to $750K by June with a 3% increase in expenses.

The four-step goal process is as follows:

1 Commitment – from yourself and then others
2 Bite-size manageable chunks
3 Measurable with a target date
4 Action plan for each goal

Until you translate your goals into actions, they have no value. A goal is not something you actually do. Instead, you complete individual action steps to achieve your desired outcome.

Projects are the ideal way to organize your goals and the ideal way to frame your work. Table 7.2 presents a project framework template.

Table 7.2 Project framework template

Generating client referrals	Developing new markets	Expanding service existing client
1. Goal	1. Goal	1. Goal
2. Goal	2. Goal	2. Goal
3. Goal	3. Goal	3. Goal
4. Goal	4. Goal	4. Goal
5. Goal	5. Goal	5. Goal

How do I implement this?

The three laws of goal setting are as follows:

1   You don't complete a goal.
2   You complete the action steps.
3   Goals are best broken down into smaller, short-term bite-size goals.

Create a project for each of your goals.

Top performer perspective

Ward Dedman, CEO, EBM Insurance

When did EBM commence?

EBM started in 1975 in Perth, Western Australia.

How many employees?

We have between 260 and 270 employees.

What services does EBM provide?

We have three core businesses: broking, risk advisory business, and our landlord's business. In addition, we have Cover Link, an internal service provider for our brokerage teams.

How do you pursue your business goals?

Once upon a time, we're probably chasing all trying to be all things to all people, but in the past couple of years we've broken down our client base into sectors and tried to understand what those segments are and what they need. So, we're probably playing to what we think are our real strengths and not trying to chase everything that moves.

My time in the field

Goal setting and discipline (Chapter 4) go hand in hand. I recommend setting your own growth goals over and above what your business is asking and use discipline to achieve these. By following this practice, you will acquire good habits and always be ahead of the game. Aim to work ahead of your targets, by maintaining a strong pipeline of qualified prospects.

Key takeaways

- Goals are statements of measurable results to be achieved. They become your route marker that provides you with a track to run on.
- Done properly, goal setting is more than just setting numbers. It should include where you need to focus your efforts and the strategies to help you translate your wishes into reality.
- Anytime you elect to pursue one goal instead of another, you have made a priority decision.
- Reducing a goal to a manageable or bite size makes it possible to achieve almost any achievable goal.
- Until you translate your goals into actions, they have no value.

Note

1   Lewis Carroll, Alice in Wonderland.

Chapter 8

H – Habits

Acquiring the tools for success

What are habits?

Top performers continually develop good habits to become more productive than average performers. On the contrary, average performers constantly develop habits that hinder their performance. If you want to produce better results, then you must do things differently, and doing these things must become a habit.

Habits are a constructive way of meeting the challenges of life mentally in an economical way of dealing with routine activities, such as sales, marketing, prospecting, and those that are essential to sales. Success is the formation of good habits and attitudes.

Habits include both attitudes and actions, for example, habits of thought and emotional responses. It's important for your sales success that you form success, attitudes, enthusiasm, determination, these all mental and emotional habits that are distinguished from actions, and you must understand that such an internal habit controls your overt actions.

Why are habits important?

The biggest secret of top professionals' sales success is consistency. That's why developing good habits is so important. If you can develop these habits in yourself, you'll stay focused on what's important and set yourself up for an amazing career in sales.

Your success in sales will depend not on the tactics you execute periodically, but on the habits you develop continually. Stand-alone goals and isolated incidents won't help you nearly as much as cultivating a cohesive, repeatable process. Spend time reinforcing good habits throughout your workday and in your deeper sales philosophy. Eventually, those positive habits will pay off big (see Figure 8.1).

DOI: 10.4324/9781003364580-9

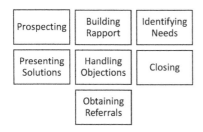

Figure 8.1 The seven sales habits required for success.

What are sales habits?

Finding ideal clients

Top professionals think about prospecting most of the time. You must develop the habit of spending more time with better prospects and looking for new business 80% of the time.

Your goal is to build an overflowing pipeline filled with your ideal clients.

Building relationships

Focus on building relationships. People buy from you first and then from your firm. Take as much time as necessary to build trust and rapport. Ask good questions and listen to understand a prospect's needs.

Identifying needs

Asking good questions to identify needs is essential, as most prospects are not aware that they can improve their life or work situation when they first meet you.

The more questions you ask about a client's situation and link your offering to those needs, the more open the client becomes to learning and becoming educated on your offering and being converted from a prospect to a client.

Presenting

Once you have clearly identified a prospect's needs and wants, show them how your offering can satisfy and meet their expectations in a cost-effective way. It shows why it makes sense to act.

Top professionals position themselves as advisors and educators and show how they most benefit from your offering.

Handling objections

Top professionals anticipate objections in advance and think through the reasons why someone may not proceed and develop answers to each of these objections in advance.

The very best have thought through every scenario and have created bulletproof answers.

Closing

Top professionals plan the close in advance. They ask questions to ensure that there are no lingering objections. They ask the prospect to act now. The more you are confident and comfortable about prospecting at the start of the process, the better you get at closing and the better you become at every other state of the sales process. You become self-motivated.

Obtaining referrals

The habit of asking for referrals makes prospecting easier. Top professionals gain 80% of their new business from referrals from existing clients.

What are personal habits?

Imagine that you were no longer able to prospect. The only selling you could do would be to referrals you receive from your existing clients. You would have to organize your time, work, and activities in such a way that your existing clients are happy with you and happy to provide a steady stream of referrals (see Figure 8.2).

Habit of self organization

Being organized is critical for sales success. On average, people spend 1.8 hours per day searching for information that's over 9 hours per week. Top performers organize their tools and planning methods for prospecting, developing presentations, and their time schedules. Self-organization techniques will be covered fully in Chapter 19.

Figure 8.2 Seven personal traits of top performers.

Habit of being proactive

Habit of proactivity is defined as being future focus, taking responsibility to make things happen, and not waiting for prospects to come to you but taking the initiative to continually reach out. Instead of hoping a client will mention you to their colleagues in their network, regularly ask your best clients for referrals and introductions. Be prepared for every possible objection and develop clear answers well in advance so that you can operate in the moment.

Habit of being client centric

Always think about what's in the best interest of your clients. Keeping your client information up to date. Continually search for new insights, ideas, and applications to help clients address their hot-button needs and solve their most pressing issues and challenges.

Habit of leveraging relationships

There are five key relationships – clients, prospects, influencers, team/colleagues, and alliance partners. Managing these is the key to continually grow your business and capabilities as a professional. Asking for referrals from each client and providing good service lead to good referrals. When you provide service that exceeds a client's expectations, you earn the right to ask for referrals.

Habit of affiliation

Top professionals are always seeking ways to expand their networks and contacts. Regularly add new LinkedIn contacts, join, and participate in trade associations where their clients are active. Participating in new pursuits and hobbies such as tennis, golf, and wine tasting are pleasure activities; however, it also expands your intellectual breadth and helps in increasing your affiliation with people you know.

Habit of cultivation

This can be defined as becoming an ideas factory for your clients and prospects. You should have excellent logical, well-thought-out presentations on each of the benefits and value of your offering that addresses the needs of the prospect.

Habit of learning

This links to raising your knowledge bar and intellectual firepower. The best can talk on a range of subjects with clients and be conversant in lots of areas. You acquire this knowledge through reading, scanning the major newspapers, attending workshops, listening to podcast, talking to interesting people, and being curious about the world around you.

How do you replace poor habits?

If you want to produce better results, then you must do things differently and doing this new thing must become a habit.
A three-step process for replacing bad habits is as follows:

- Recognize the satisfaction that habit provides.
- Know the specific satisfaction it provides.
- Substitute more effective habits.

Conditioning your attitudes and habits may have been conditioned by environmental and association rainmakers, make it happen.
   For new businesses, there are some habits that could prevent roadblocks: fear indecision, lack of information, lack of training, refer to the learning loop Chapter 1.

How do you acquire good habits?

Habits matter. They are about becoming someone they hope you become the type of person you wish to be. Behind every system of actions is a system of beliefs.

We will unconsciously form habits that are more pleasing, but less productive. You must form new habits because if you keep conducting your affairs in the same way that you have been habitually in the past, you could only expect to get the same results. A habit is a routine or a behavior that is performed regularly and, in many ways, automatic habits are the micro actions that are part of the larger system.

Top performer perspective

Joe Arena, CEO, Procurement Australia

What habits has your organization adopted?

Walking the talk in environment sustainability, community, and governance, we have established milestones within our own organization that we have to meet.

We try to use recycled paper, otherwise being as paperless as possible. Our leadership team who all have a car space in the city are committed to catching public transport.

View from the field

Acquiring and maintaining good sales habits is essential for success. Unfortunately, too many professionals are poorly trained; this has a flown effect as the person who trained them never acquired good habits. Seek out top professionals in your company and industry and study them. I've found good salespeople are willing to share their knowledge. Invest in yourself to acquire books, courses, and attend seminars. Do whatever is necessary to acquire good sales habits and practices early and then pay it forward by sharing your knowledge with others.

Key takeaways

- If you want to produce better results, then you must do things differently and doing these things must become a habit.
- Your success in sales will depend not on the tactics you execute periodically, but on the habits you develop continually.

- Stand-alone goals and isolated incidents won't help you nearly as much as cultivating a cohesive, repeatable process.
- Spend time reinforcing good habits throughout your workday and in your deeper sales philosophy. Eventually, those positive habits will pay off big.
- You become your habits. Habits matter. They are about becoming someone they hope you become the type of person you wish to be.

Chapter 9

I – Ideas

A versatile clean four-letter word

What is an idea?

Idea is an extremely versatile and powerful four-letter word, a clean four-letter word that works wonders, opens doors, gets meetings, and closes sales. Ideas arouse curiosity and become a magnetic force of attraction. Think of all the marvels of our technology, all our modern conveniences, all we first were ideas.

Ideas are powerful in selling, helping you gain the attention of prospective clients to start the sales process. Top performers package, present, and sell their ideas.

Why are ideas important?

Ideas prevent judgment. A prospect will probably be interested in considering an idea that will offer a solution to a problem or provide some special benefits. Ideas help you market and sell within your comfort. It can remove stress when prospecting or approaching prospective clients.

The word "idea" arouses curiosity and is a powerful force of attraction, making it the perfect way to approach prospective clients. Regardless of your offering, there are ideas connected with how it's used, purchased, or valued.

Of the many offerings I've been involved with in selling, I've never known a product or service for which it does not have an idea that applies to it. Somewhere from experience with other clients or reports that you've heard from others you probably know of a unique or especially great idea in the use of your service that will help you open a door or at least get the attention of a prospective client.

> I'm constantly searching for new ideas to stay and be in better position to assist my clients.
> (Garth Lovelace, CEO, SFR Advisory Group of Companies)

DOI: 10.4324/9781003364580-10

Where do you find ideas?

Begin with the markets you are presently serving your best clients (the top 20%). To penetrate any target niche (Chapter 14) successfully, you must offer "silver bullets." These are solutions to the hot-button issues or concerns that prospects and suspects are concerned about and which a prospective client will readily meet with you to discuss how you can be of help.

Here are seven sources for generating sales ideas:

1 Monitoring conference topics
2 Reading niche market journals/newsletters
3 Annual reports
4 Newspapers
5 Speaking with industry players
6 Following the trends
7 Podcast and social media

Monitoring conference topics

Every industry and niche have a trade association representing the interest of their members. Many of these hold quarterly and annual conference meetings. Reviewing the brochure of keynotes and topics being discussed during the conference will provide insight into the important issues of the members.

Reading niche market journals and newsletters

Besides conferences, many trade associations provide a weekly and monthly newsletter for its members available electronically. I subscribe to *Insurance News*, which produces a daily news bulletin and monthly magazine that is free to subscribe. By scanning the headlines and articles, I can quickly stay up to date on industry issues.

Annual reports

Public companies must produce an annual report that provides a wealth of insightful niche market information. Most annual reports are available online for free. Start by identifying the public companies serving your niche. The important pages to read are the chairperson's report and CEO's report at the front. They will outline the challenges, hot-button issues, opportunities, and problems they are currently facing.

Newspapers

Major newspapers such as the *Wall Street Journal, Guardian, Daily Mail,* and your local papers regularly feature company stories and profiles that contain valuable information to help you develop an idea for your market. I read the *Wall Street Journal* on my IPad daily to pick up fresh ideas.

Speaking to key industry players

Seek the key players in your industry and markets. These don't have to be the CEO. I recently spoke to a mid-level hotel manager who shared her frustrations the industry is facing in attracting and keeping talent. A smart recruiter could easily develop some ideas to approach to assist them.

Following trends

Engaging in any of the above activities will help identify hot-button issues and key trends, a general direction in which something is taking place. Some current trends include artificial intelligence, Adtech, Fintech, and the human experience when going digital.

Podcast and social media

Listening to industry and news podcast is a great way to grab information when you are on the move. On social media sites such as LinkedIn, you can follow product announcements and make new connections to expand your network.

How do you sell with ideas?

Getting in the habit of asking good questions (Chapter 17) focuses on learning, not selling. Good questions are the building blocks to get to the heart of what a prospective client really wants. Begin searching for ideas with your existing clients by asking about:

- What are they excited about?
- What do they fear or need to eliminate?
- What are they confident about?
- What are they struggling with?
- What challenges are they facing?

These types of questions and their answers will help uncover a problem or hot-button issues that a client is facing, which need to be addressed. Always look for new and useful questions that make you more skillful at helping people identify actions they need to achieve their goals.

Create specific ideas around the problems you find and keep them simple and make them easy to understand. The great Ben Feldman writes, "create small simple clean packages and the simpler the better when something made simple, it was easy for him to understand." This resulted in him selling millions and millions of dollars worth of insurance products.

The key to a sale is the idea and the key to selling the idea is to package it. It can be the idea that will make the prospect earn more money, cut costs, and do a job more easily, faster, or whatever. Show prospects and clients ideas that will help solve their problems and concerns.

The idea is free. It opens doors and gets meetings. The idea has to do with an intangible benefit. Using the word "idea" forces you to do something it takes your mind off what you are selling and center it on what it will do the prospect. Your idea is a client-focused approach to market your offerings.

Conduct an annual review with your existing clients using the above questions to uncover their needs. Once you've mastered the client conversation, start asking good questions of your prospects. Your first meeting with a prospect should be a strategic interview, where the prospect talks most of the time. The skillful use of probing questions will help uncover the needs and buying preferences.

How do you package your ideas?

Listen and think and keep working on your ideas until they are solid and backed up with proof that relates to a prospect's self-interest. Your ideas should address a prospect's challenges, struggles, concerns, and dangers.

Focus on the need and benefit you can provide rather than pitching your product or serving your offer. You should package your ideas by creating a name that both positions the idea in the market and defines the core value of benefit.

There are three types of ideas:

1 To eliminate a fear or danger
2 To take advantage of an opportunity
3 To maximize or leverage a strength

Top performer perspective

Simon Swanston, CEO, ClearView

How do you encourage new ideas in your business?

Any member of our leadership can call a meeting to explore an idea or opportunity. These sometimes last for two to three hours.

Time in the field

Marketing with ideas allows you to work from your comfort zone. It's like fishing with bait, you present an idea and when a prospect bites you can arrange to have an in-depth discussion to explore the idea further and see if they qualify. This is a professional and ethical way to market yourself and your offerings. Any offering can be turned into an idea, when categorize your ideas, it provides a valid reason to remain in touch with prospects by presenting new ideas and information.

Top professionals are seen as thought leaders in their fields and for their inights and it all begins with having valuable ideas and information to share with prospective clients.

Key takeaways

- "Idea" is an extremely versatile and powerful four-letter word, a clean four-letter word that works wonders, opens doors, gets meetings, and closes sales.
- Ideas are powerful in selling, helping you to gain the attention of pro- spective clients.
- Using ideas helps you to market and sell within your comfort zone. It can remove stress when prospecting or approaching prospective clients.
- Create specific ideas around the problems you find and keep them simple and make them easy to understand.
- Focus on the need and benefit you can provide rather than pitching your product or serving your offer.

Chapter 10

J – Jargon

Understanding market buzzwords

What is jargon?

Jargon is the special language used within a profession. Every industry and occupation spanning from medicine, law, finance, education, engineering, construction trades, and more have their own language and their own unique vocabulary.

Learning the language can benefit you as a seller when you learn the language of that industry. It's a formal language used in niche markets and a common shorthand used sensibly for quick, efficient communication.

Plumbers use terms such as *elbow*, *ABS*, *sweating the pipes*, *reduced*, *flapper*, *snake*, and *rough-in*. Other plumbers and suppliers understand those terms in plumbing, but to non-plumbers, those terms may have different meanings.

Jargon differs from slang, which is informal language in conversations, text messages, and other social communication among friends.

Why is jargon important?

Having an insider understanding refers to your in-depth knowledge of how the niche works, and what it takes to make a profit. When marketing your offering, in order to be seen as an insider you need to learn the industry structure and dynamics. Top performers become industry insiders by learning the special language in that market.

I do a lot of work in the financial services industry. The common terms that I come across include:

- Renewal revenue – percentage of revenue retained from existing clients
- Combined ratio – the incurred losses and expenses in relation to the total collected premiums
- Organic growth – growth in revenues from the previous year
- AE – account executives
- CSR – customer service representative

DOI: 10.4324/9781003364580-11

When I speak to finance executives using this language, it quickly establishes my credibility as an industry insider, and they feel comfortable discussing the goals and objectives and listening to some ideas to address their pressing needs.

What advantages does jargon provide?

When you understand and speak the language of your target market, marketing becomes easier to produce provocatively written communication describing your services on your website, prospecting emails, writing newsletters and articles, proposals, and phone calls.

I once met a gentleman at a networking event. I asked him what line of work he was in, and he responded, "I'm an education consultant." I asked what that means? He gave a lengthy explanation that left me no clearer. If I was a potential buyer for his services, I would have trouble understanding his offering and value.

It was no surprise when he mentioned a few minutes later that he was finding business difficult.

Where do you find jargon for an industry?

Even if you work in a highly specialized market (Chapter 14), do not overuse industry jargons – keep your language broad when marketing, don't assume that everyone is a specialist.

Use jargon sparingly during these occasions:

- Sharing your value proposition
- On your website
- Voice mail messages
- Prospecting emails
- Proposals

Having an insider understanding of an industry refers to your in-depth knowledge of how the niche market works. Here are five industry data sources:

1 Local library
2 Industry trade associations
3 Talking with clients and industry key players
4 Google
5 Networking and attending conferences

Go deep with the internet

The internet is like an iceberg. Less than 10% information is available on the surface. The remaining 90% comprises the deep web with information stored in databases that are accessible by subscriptions, including:

- Dun and Bradstreet
- IBIS reports

How do you use jargon?

When you engage in occupational networking, for example, with industry trade associations, using jargon can helps create a powerful marketing message to package and position your expertise with prospective clients.

Emails

Using email is an efficient way to market and follow up prospective clients. Use jargon in prospecting emails to help you share your ideas and gain the attention and land meetings. And you write targeted emails using the right language and they gain the attention of prospective clients, making it easy to secure meetings and appointments.

Here is an example of a generic email to get an appointment.

Example of a generic approach

Subject line: Organic growth ideas

Bob,

I'm writing you to introduce our company Acme performance.

We provide sales training to companies to help them land and keep new customers. I would like the opportunity to meet with you to discuss your needs and how we can help you grow your business.

If we can be of service to you anytime, please call me on (916) 427-3228. I look forward to hearing from you.

Regards,
Mary B.

What's wrong with this approach? For a busy decision-maker, it does not provide an interesting reason to meet. It does not show if you have expertise in his market industry.

Example of an effective approach

Bob,

Congratulations on your recent merger with ABC finance.

During the past seven, I have provided extensive help to the general insurance focusing on the acquisition, development, and retention of commercial clients.

I have a few ideas on dramatically improving organic growth without increasing sales acquisition cost you may find interesting.

Would make sense for us to meet briefly?

Regards,
Mary B.

What makes this email effective?
   It speaks about their specific industry; it uses language (jargon) that the decision-maker will immediately recognize, such as organic growth, retention, and acquisition of new business and provides a nonthreatening; the next step that makes it easy for the decision-maker to respond.

Proposal writing

We can use jargon in writing proposals and when responding to an request for a proposal (RFP), request for a proposal to simple one-page proposals. It helps to show and package your understanding of that niche market and stand out from the competition.

What are some common industry terms?

Below are some common sales and marketing terms used in business. You don't have to use all these words at once – there *is* such a thing as too many buzzwords. Instead, start with just a few words and phrases at a time. Occasionally working them into your presentations can make them tasteful additions to your meetings.

ARR

Annual Recurring Revenue. For recurring revenue companies.

B2B

Business 2 Business.

B2C

Business 2 Consumer.

Benefit

The value of a product or service that a consumer of that product or service experiences.

BANT

An acronym used in sales for lead qualification that stands for Budget, Authority, Need, and Timeline.

Buyer persona

A representation of your ideal customer.

Buying criteria

All the information a consumer needs to make a buying decision.

Buying process/cycle

The process potential buyers go through before deciding whether to make a purchase.

Churn rate

A metric that measures how many customers you retain and at what value.

Closed opportunities

An umbrella term that includes both closed-won and closed-lost opportunities.

Closed-won

When a sales representative closes a deal in which the buyer purchases the product or service.

Closed-lost

When a sales representative closes a deal in which the buyer does not purchase the product or service.

Closing ratio

The percentage of prospects that someone successfully close-wins.

Cold calling

Making unsolicited calls.

Cross-selling

Selling additional services to existing clients.

Customer acquisition cost

Total sales and marketing cost.

Customer relationship management (CRM)

Software that let companies keep track of everything they do with their existing and potential customers.

Decision-maker

The person who, or role that, makes the final decision of a sale.

Discovery call

Asking prospects questions to qualify.

Feature

A function of a product that can solve a potential buyer's need.

Forecasting

Estimating future sales performance for a forecast period based on historical data.

Gatekeeper

A person who, or role that, enables or prevents information from getting to another person(s) in a company.

Lead

A person or company who has shown interest in a product or service.

Lifetime value

A prediction of the net profit attributed to the entire future relationship with a client.

   The amount is added to the cost price of goods to cover overhead and profit.

Net promoter score

A customer satisfaction metric.

Objection

A prospect's challenge or question for additional information.

Opportunity

A qualified lead.

Pain point

A prospect's pain point, or need.

Pipeline

The step-by-step process sales representatives go through to convert a prospect into a client.

Positioning statement

Statements and questions to engage a prospect in conversation.

Profit margin

A ratio of profitability.

Prospecting

Searching for and finding potential buyers.

Qualified lead

A prospect who has shown interest in your product or service.

Sales methodology

A framework of actionable steps during each stage of the sales process.

Social selling

Using social media to interact directly with their prospects.

Sound bite

A series of words or phrases to respond to and overcome a customer objection.

Stage

Parts of the sales pipeline representing each step in the sales process.

Top of the funnel

The very first stage of the buying process.

Up-selling

Selling an existing client a higher-end version of your product or service.

Value proposition

A benefit of a product or company intended to make it more attractive to potential buyers.

Weighted pipeline

A more detailed version of a sales pipeline.

Become familiar with the common sales terms and how to apply them to your business, you'll be able to better converse with prospects and clients about their business.

Top performer perspective

Joe Arena, CEO Procurement, Australia

How do you incorporate industry buzzwords?

Well in our industry it's all about the procurement function and agility. We have to be agile and be ready and dynamic enough to quickly change with whatever the client needs or whatever the market is doing.

What are some common buzzwords or jargon?

Because we deal with government a lot, what we hear about most is diversity, social procurement, sustainability, and education there. We've made them our four pillars because we need to maintain a focus on that so that our government clients can see that we are dedicated to their cause.

View from the field

Taking the time to learn the language can dramatically shorten the sales cycle and eliminate the competition. You have demonstrated to your buyer that you've done your homework and know your stuff.

Key takeaways

- Jargon is the special language used within a profession, every industry and occupation.
- It's a formal language used in niche markets – a common shorthand used sensibly for quick, efficient communication.
- Having an insider understanding refers to your in-depth knowledge of how the niche works and what it takes to make a profit.
- Do not overuse industry jargon – keep your language broad when marketing, don't assume that everyone is a specialist.

Chapter 11

K – Knowledge

Getting smart about selling

What is sales knowledge?

Sales professionals know what they sell, and they sell what they know. Too often prfessionals know very little about their industry niche markets, client needs, and their firms offering to sell. Without this knowledge, they cannot be successful, such as asking the right questions to uncover a prospect's needs, matching the right offering to those needs, positioning their value of their company against competitors, and holding masterful sales conversations with clients.

This results in lost sales and missed cross-selling opportunities.

BJ is a rainmaker for an accounting firm, he does a great job attracting prospective clients, establishing trust and credibility, converting them into paid clients. His client retention rate is 98% and 80% most of his new business generated from referrals from existing clients. BJ maintains an overflowing pipeline of qualified regarding regardless of the market or the economy.

BJ does not consider himself a salesperson; he is a technical person who has learned how to sell, and he's developed his sales capabilities to where he enjoys marketing and selling is firm's offerings.

Professionals like BJ are salespeople, knowledge workers with specialized skills who enjoy solving expensive problems for their clients. They consistently upgrade their knowledge formally and informally with regard to selling, marketing clients, and other general areas.

What's the difference between knowledge and skills training?

There are two types of training required to be successful in sales. The first is knowledge and the second is skills. Many professionals and organizations make the mistake of confusing the two.

DOI: 10.4324/9781003364580-12

Legendary insurance professional John Savage once said his technical skills only contributed 5% to his success, the other 95% he attributed to his people skills. The trick is you have to have 100% of the 5%. For most top professionals the technical aspects (products knowledge) account for 20% and people skills contribute 80%.

Knowledge and skills training are two separate things. Knowledge is learning the science of what there is to know about your products and services and offering. An insurance professional needs to learn about different risk products, underwriting, claims, and compliance.

Sales skills training combines informal knowledge based on your practical experience in the field dealing with prospects and clients. It's your ideas, observations, and experiences that can add value to a buyer with general business knowledge.

Avoid the mistake of pretending that even the best education will make you a good sales professional. The methods used are different. Knowledge training is formal learning in the classroom and skills training is about getting into the field of selling comfortably.

I believe that any person who is naturally bright can learn anything and everything there is to know to be successful, including the habits, tools, and traits. However, you can't learn to deal with such as fear simply through book knowledge. Ultimately, experience is the best teacher.

What is continual learning?

Don't make the mistake of stopping your learning after reaching a plateau that you consider as successful. You need to keep pushing yourself to set a higher standard. Always be on the lookout for fresh ideas and insights to better serve your clients and market.

Attend conferences and association meetings with a receptive mind and be smart enough to walk away with things that will help you. By Staying active in your niche markets, attending conferences and reading trade journals you will pick up new ideas (Chapter 10) to approach prospective clients. (Chapter 21).

Take charge of your own training and development

Top professionals don't wait for their company to provide personal development. They practice and prepare in advance. When you enter a buyer's office, you are ready and prepared to discuss your value offering.

When you meet a prospective buyer, they expect you to understand their business, direction, challenges, processes, and relationship, and they expect you to do your homework before you get there. With today's technology, there's no reason that you can't achieve that. Buyers want your ideas, insights, leadership, and guidance to access whatever change makes sense and how they can best do that.

Provide prospective clients with what they need, when they want it, and how they want it quickly. Invest your time, learning about the business, track trends, and investigate your clients and prospects. Go deep on your level of insights, understand innovation, and think about "client centric" (Chapter 3).

What knowledge areas do I need?

Your contiunued success in your depends on you knowing more, providing value, and meeting buyers where they are. Today's buyers are self-educated, often leaving sellers out in the loop. When they have an issue, they go online, research their problems, check websites, and look up for information that can help them. They download special reports and podcasts when they're ready, and often are up to 60% of the way through the buying process when you contact them.

> Buyers are smarter today and very educated, most of them including first time home buyers have already done their homework on the internet.
> (Kathleen Beck, Mortgage Banker)

There are six broad skills and capabilities that professionals need to develop a healthy pipeline:

1 Client interviewing
2 Problem diagnostic
3 Solution development
4 Communication
5 Sales proposal development
6 Project management

Audit of your skills and capabilities

The most important habit you can develop is looking forward and identifying the skills and competencies you will need to be at the top of your field.

To grow as a sales professional, keep yourself up with both the knowledge of your services and selling. Knowledge is the combination of facts, information, and skills gained through your experience.

Professionals must develop their capabilities when relationship with buyers in selling are undergoing a radical transformation. The buyers today know more and can access information quicker. Knowledge is important to prove any skill. The first step is an honest appraisal of where you are now. Assess where you stand today by checking off each item on the checklist of your audit. Educational power lies in the application of knowing. Knowing the basics of effective selling is relatively easy to learn.

Top performer perspective

Richard Crawford, CEO, CBN

How do you stay informed about your business?

To stay informed about our business, we need two things: first, we listen and, second, we create space and time to deal with new information. We have over 900 community members. We have monthly stand-ups with their members and quarterly half-day meetings.

We conduct broker council forums and we listen to them about what's happening in their business. We learn either what they're directly telling us or what they're experiencing and what that means for us.

With respect to our own business, during COVID-19, we implemented a series of forums to short-circuit the point-to-point communication. We created communication centers where people could come to, and we also have an ideas hub.

View from the field

I recommend reading outside your field the *Wall Street Journal* everyday along with your local newspaper. Listen to podcast both in and outside your industry. Have wide interest of sports and hobbies to learn new things. Volunteer with Rotary, Lions, school PTA, the Red Cross, and coach little league. By engaging in wide activities you will meet new people and learn from them. You will increase your knowledge of how a variety of things work.

I like to build models as a hobby on several occasions during a Zoom call a buyer will ask me about one of my models that can generats a whole new discussion, further cementing our relationship.

Key takeaways

- Sales professionals know what they sell, and they sell what they know.
- There are two types of training required for becoming successful in sales. The first is knowledge and the second is skills training.
- Too many professionals and organizations make the mistake of confusing the two.
- Sales skills training combines informal knowledge based on your practical experience in the field dealing with prospects and clients.
- The most important habit you can develop is the habit of looking forward three to five years and identifying additional skills and competencies that you will need.

Chapter 12

L – Listening

Be all ears

What is listening?

Think of listening as the other side of a question. Unless the asker listens, the questions have no meaning or value. Communication is a two-way street and in oral communication, listening is 50% of the action.

Good listening takes awareness and is a critical part of the sales process and something that is not often taught in many books or classes. Comprehensive listening includes using your eyes, body language, reflective comments, and note-taking.

An effective sales technique is based on communication, everyone appreciates a good listener. In the selling process, listening is just as important as talking. When you listen, you always learn something. There is a wonderful expression that especially applies to selling: you have two ears and one mouth use them in that proportion. You can't do much listening when you're doing most of the talking. To become a better listener, cut back on the number of times you speak.

Another aspect of listening is that you must understand how a prospect thinks and feels, otherwise you cannot properly service or connect with them. This can only achieve through listening.

The natural inclination for sellers is to be thinking of what you're going to say next and if you're not careful, you are apt to miss something of what's being said or worse; the prospect is likely to sense that you are not listening and paying attention.

We have four four actuaries who work our business they are working on the data analytics all the time. That's the sophistication that's come into insurance much more, I would say over the last two decades around the world. I used to say to insurers who are burning their loss ratio in

DOI: 10.4324/9781003364580-13

certain sections, why don't you get some accurates? And they would reply, we've got four, and I'd say, why don't you listen to them?

(Robert Kelly, CEO, Steadfast)

What is active listening?

Active listening is allowing someone to speak without interrupting, not doing anything, and yet really paying attention to what is being said. Too often sales professionals are so busy thinking about what they want to say next that you're not actually listening to what a prospective client is saying.

Research suggests that we only recall 25%–50% of what we hear. In a 20-minute conversation, a prospect may only remember about the first 10 minutes of what you've discussed.

Active listening significantly changes how much we remember from what we hear. This is because it requires you to not just focus on what is being spoken, but the message that's being conveyed.

Active listening occurs when you fully engage in what is being said or what they are listening to. This is the process through which you can fully receive information from another person or a group of people. When you are listening actively, you have 100% of your attention on the conversation at hand. You take the time to understand what is being said and don't interrupt others when they're speaking.

When you listen actively, you are attempting to listen to gain an understanding of what is being said and the feeling behind it. You show your listening by your gestures and facial expressions demonstrating you are interested in what it's being said, looking at the person talking to you.

Resist any temptation to shift your gaze, however, don't stare. Think of active listening as a practice of preparing to listen, observing what verbal and nonverbal messages are being sent, and providing appropriate feedback for the sake of showing attentiveness to the message being presented.

What is passive listening?

Passive listening is when you are hearing someone or something without putting 100% of your attention toward listening. This is a type of communication that is pretty one-sided. The professional listening passively will often not give any feedback on what they are listening to or a client or prospect.

Listening passively does not require much effort at all. All that is happening is the listener is hearing what is being said. Sometimes, you might not even catch all of what is being said because you have not given your attention to the prospect.

Passive listening with a prospective client isn't just unproductive, it's also rude. It can make the prospect feel like what they're saying isn't of value, and it can also mean that important information isn't being fully communicated.

What is paraphrasing?

When you actively listen, you may choose to paraphrase what a prospect has said after they finished their statement. This can be incredibly valuable. It shows that you're engaged and listening.

If a person is sharing important information and you want to show that you heard them and clarify their main points, paraphrasing what they said can be a great active listening tool that benefits everyone involved.

Paraphrasing is defined as reshaping a prospect's statement with words that will reveal the unexpected meaning and feelings laid behind the original statement. Sometimes a paraphrase can clarify the language. To paraphrase, focus on listening, identify the feelings beneath the words and try to fill in the blank spaces with what's being omitted, and reduce or eliminate vague statements. Paraphrasing also is important when handling objections and client concerns.

When you actively listen to a prospect, feeding back their words by paraphrasing them shows that you have listened, and they'll provide clarity or correct you on anything that you might have missed.

What about note-taking?

Note-taking and listening go hand in hand. The mind is a lousy place to store information, it's not a computer. Taking notes during a conversation is important to show that you have been listening. Take notes of the key points, ideas, questions, and summaries and use this with regard to paraphrase and clarity.

Note-taking and listening are important when you're putting together elements for a proposal or taking the next actions that you want a prospective client to take. With complex selling situations, there are many steps and sometimes several meetings before a sale is closed.

By taking accurate notes, and updating your contact management system you are setting the stage for the next meeting, but to do that, you need to listen.

How do you handle ramblers?

These are people that go on and on. Sometimes their stories or statements are not relevant to the discussion. The best way to deal with a rambler is to avoid showing impatience, wait for them to complete their thought, or break into their monologue, and then direct the conversation back toward your aim.

You may occasionally have to do this several times, however it keeps you in control of the sales conversation. Be aware how often you speak compared to the amount of time you listen during a conversation.

Top performer perspective

Ward Dedman, CEO, EBM Insurance

How do you practice listening in your business?

We are always talking to our clients to learn and understand their problems, challenges, and opportunities. Internally in our business, continuous communication and team meetings are required so that everyone understands where we are going as a business. We spend a lot of time and effort ensuring that our internal communications link everything together so that people can actually realize that they're just not here doing a job.

We (the leadership team) listen so that we understand what's meaningful for everyone across the business; this sometimes can be challenging, we operate from ten locations across the country. I think just keeping everyone connected with where we're going, and why we are doing it is one of the most important contributions I made as a CEO.

View from the field

Don't be afraid of the silence when a prospect is responding to a question; there may be silence when they stop and you feel necessary to fill the void with another question. Wait a few more seconds, the prospect may be gathering his thoughts and may provide additional details to your initial answer. Some prospects speak slowly, don't be tempted to interrupt or correct. When you sit back and listen, you may be rewarded with valuable information to help you close the sale and win a new client.

Key takeaways

- Think of listening as the other side of a question.
- Good listening takes awareness and is a critical part of the sales process.
- An effective sales technique is based on communication, and communication is a two-way street, and everyone appreciates a good listener.
- Active listening is allowing someone to speak without interrupting, not doing anything, and yet not really paying attention to what is being said.
- Note-taking and listening go hand in hand.
- The best way to deal with the rambler is to avoid showing impatience, When you encounter a rambler, you may need to wait for the right time break into their monologue, and then direct the conversation back toward your aim.

Chapter 13

M – Marketing

Promoting and selling your offering

What is marketing?

Marketing is about attracting your ideal client; it starts by gaining their attention and interest that provide an opportunity to obtain a meeting. In selling intangible services, marketing is finding an organized approach to find an interest point in the mind of a prospective client. It's a way of thinking about your market and what's important to prospective clients and packaging, promoting your expertise.

Why is marketing important?

Finding and keeping a core group of clients is the bread and butter of any business. Targeting and attracting clients is far from simple increasingly crowded and competive markets.

When you are just starting out, you may need to spend as much as 80% of your time on marketing using a combination of direct and indirect approaches. Seasoned professionals still spend 25%–40% of their time on marketing using a combination of direct and indirect methods to attract prospects.

A strong pipeline of qualified leads is the key to producing superior growth results regardless of the economy or market conditions. Good marketing ensures you have a steady stream of new leads to continue feeding your pipeline.

I recommend four marketing strategies:

1 Specializing
2 Differentiating
3 Knowing your ideal client
4 Focusing your sales efforts

DOI: 10.4324/9781003364580-14

Specializing

Professionals who specialize find it easier to attract, keep, and develop long-term client relationships. Specializing includes identifying, penetrating, and developing one to three niche markets (Chapter 14), to become a professional with a deep level of experience and expertise.

Differentiating

This is your competitive advantage, describing why your offering is superior to that of your competitors; without this, your offering can be viewed as a commodity, making it difficult for prospective clients to tell the difference between competitors.

Knowing your ideal client

Many people might purchase your offering; however, they are not all prospective clients for you. Segment your clients into A, B, and C categories – determine who the top 20% are that produce most of your revenue. List their traits and characteristics and focus on attracting more of these types of prospects.

Focus

Focus most of your time and effort on sales-related activities (Chapter 20) attracting, acquiring, developing, and keeping your top 20% clients. Filter down your universe of prospects to maximize your return on time and energy invested.

What are the 5Ps?

Some view marketing as promotion; others think of it as selling. Still others consider it to be one's business identity, while each of these is important. The 5Ps simply make sense out of all of these elements and put them into a logical order (Figure 13.1).

Positioning

Positioning is your marketing message and it answers the following questions:

- What exactly is your business solution?
- How does your offering solve a particular problem, alleviate a pain, or add value?

Figure 13.1 The 5Ps of marketing.

- Who are your targeted potential clients?
- What differentiates you from your competitors?
- What results can clients expect?

Packaging

This expresses your identity and positioning verbally and in written form showing:

- The problems, issues, and challenges your clients are dealing with.
- Your services, what you do, and how you do it.
- You present your business in a way that truly represents who you are.

Promotion

The purpose of promotion is to get the phone ringing with highly qualified prospective clients on the line including:

- A systematic referral process
- Communicating your expertise through speaking and networking within your target market
- Keeping touch regularly with newsletters and published articles

Persuasion

This means converting prospects into clients with the following:

- Building rapport
- Skillful use of questioning to learn about their situation
- Closing, asking for the business

Performance

It is defined as meeting a client's expectations and going the extra mile and ultimately creating Raving Fans:

- Doing everything in your power to deliver a service that consistently exceeds clients' expectations.
- Staying motivated and true to the personal vision of your business.
- Getting things done, not only for your clients, but also for yourself to make your business successful.

What is indirect versus direct marketing?

Direct marketing

There are people you know and have met, including clients, past clients, prospects, family, friends, previous colleagues, and associates, basically everyone you know. Top professionals continually focus on expanding their network formally and informally. Direct marketing allows you to work from your comfort zone with people who already know you and trust you.

Use a systematic approach to stay in touch using email, cards, reminders, articles, newsletters, and holiday and birthday cards throughout the year – educating and reminding them of your value . This is one of the most effective and fastest methods to generate new business, leads, introductions, and referrals.

Indirect marketing

There are people who do not know you or you have not met. The aim of indirect marketing is to move into these people into your inner circle of your network and nurture them through direct marketing. Indirect marketing is effective when you have identified your niche markets (Chapter 14). This is marketing to the masses to get a trivial few. Use speaking, networking Send out a monthly newsletter. Top real estate agents generate a 50:1 conversation rate with indirect marketing.

Top professionals use a mix of these approaches throughout their career to keep the pipeline fresh with qualified leads.

What is an ideal client?

Your marketing needs to be focused on the right areas to provide the highest return on your time and energy invested. Marketing is not a numbers game spending hours on the phone cold calling or hoping to find someone to meet you; it's about packaging your expertise to gain the attention of someone with a hot-button need and that starts by understanding your ideal client (Table 13.1).

Client profile chart is about matching your expertise to a prospective clients problems and/or opportunities your ideal clients include:

Demographics: size, revenue or number of employee's.

Psychographics: their attitudes, values, and belief.

Awards for excellence are all good examples of psychographics.

Geographic: where are they located – local, national, or international, or a combination thereof?

How do you package your expertise?

There are two ways to package your expertise: verbal and written (including electronic) and you need both.

Table 13.1 Ideal client worksheet

Segment	Example	Notes
Demographics	• Industry • Size • Revenue • Customers • Processes	
Geographic	• Local • Regional • National • International	
Psychographics	• Vision • Values • Beliefs • Reputation • Perception	

Types of written expertise packages include:

- List of your services
- Types of clients you serve
- Case studies
- Articles and special reports
- Testimonials
- Website

Five ways to use your written expertise:

1 Prospecting and speaking opportunities
2 In your sales kit
3 On your website
4 Social media (LinkedIn)
5 Providing follow-up information

What is a verbal message?

Your verbal message describes what you do when you are asked to do when networking, informally and formally meeting people. A good verbal message conveys to prospective clients why they should work with you – it's also the foundation for an efficient voicemail.

There are four ways to talk about what you do:

1 Your label
2 Your process
3 Your expertise
4 Their problem

Your label – job description

When asked what you do? "I'm an engineer or I'm an accountant" or "I'm a doctor." This is how the majority of people introduce themselves to your job description.

Your process

This is your methodology, what you do, focus instead on your outcomes when answering the question what you do.

Your expertise

This is much better. In fact, in many situations this works fine as it at least talks about a benefit.

Their problem

People are much more interested, not in you and your stuff but themselves and their stuff. The purpose of your solution is to solve their problem. So why not talk about their problem first? You can take every one of the verbal messages as stated above and turn them around.

Marketing is about creating need and a mindset to people. Satisfy their hot-button needs.

Top performer perspective

Bernie McIntosh, Managing Director, Victorian Mortgage Group

Who is the target market?

Mortgage and finance brokers who need assistance with the types of loans we provide. When an opportunity comes crosses their desk, they immediately try to arrange funding with a bank. the bank declines When the deal, they need a friendly helping hand to help them to set up the loan and we work alongside them to assist them in that regard. This really gives us an edge in the marketplace. We conduct workshops and work on building relationships with brokers to help make their jobs easier.

View from the field

Top professionals proactively market themselves to attract their ideal clients by gaining their attention. This is key to generating a steady stream of opportunities. The best marketing approach is one that allows you to work from your comfort zone. Start by leveraging your existing clients, providing great service, and regularly asking for referrals (Chapter 18) working with center of influences in your chosen niche markets for introductions. When you are just starting, the majority of your marketing should be 80% direct where you are going to the market. The long-term goal is to develop your marketing into 80% indirect approach with prospective clients contacting you.

Key takeaways

- Marketing is about attracting your ideal client; it starts by gaining their attention and interest that provide an opportunity.
- Finding and keeping a core group of clients is the bread and butter of any business.
- Professionals who specialize find it easier to attract, keep, and develop long-term client relationships.
- Differentiation is your competitive advantage, describing why your offering is superior to that of your competitors.

Chapter 14

N – Niche

Becoming someone special

What is a niche market?

The key to predictable growth is to be seen as someone special to special group of people. You achieve that by identifying markets that match your needs, capabilities, and passion and being received as being different and better.

The first step is to identify the markets you want to focus on. You cannot be all things to all people, and you certainly can't be all things to all clients.

> I think once upon a time, we were probably trying to be all things to all people, but in the last few years we've broken our client base down into sectors to better understand what we believe they need.
> (Ward Dedman, CEO, EBM Insurance)

Why niche marketing?

It's one of the most effective ways to market and sell while working in your comfort zone, and you don't have to cold call anymore.

Every market requires a high level of expertise and experience to capture it effectively. The more you understand the dynamics of a particular market, the easier it is to get meetings with prospective clients and generate referrals.

Niche marketing forms the elements of an effective marketing action plan. This is your playbook of ideas, approaches to prospective clients, scripts, and list of names of prospects and key influencers. The key to effective niche marketing is walking the talk by putting your plans into action and providing your credibility, visibility, and building trust.

DOI: 10.4324/9781003364580-15

How do you select a niche?

Choosing an industry niche market(s) is one of the most strategic decisions you can make regarding the long-term viability in your business. You are probably already working in one or more niche market without realizing it.

I once worked with a client with a major account in the transportation industry that was generating 40% of the revenues for the business. The client was worried about having all their "eggs" in one basket.

I was surprised to learn this client only had one client in the transportation sector. It never occurred to them to seek other companies that could benefit from their expertise. The best way to identify a niche market is to follow the "money trail" within your client's existing base.

The goal is to develop an insider understanding of how each of your chosen markets work by locating data sources, determining the structure and nature of the industry.

There are five questions to ask when selecting a niche market:

1 What primary markets do we presently serve?
2 What secondary markets do we serve?
3 Are these markets growing?
4 Do we enjoy serving these markets?
5 Are there a significant number of players in the market?

Buyers believe that their circumstances are unique and they want to work with a professional who has both expertise and experience and is working with people like them. When you focus on niche markets, you will reduce your competition because many professionals operate as generalists and don't develop the deep level of expertise required.

How do you become the go-to person?

Niche marketing is an important part of your professional development as well as new business development for your firm. You'll gain confidence in your ability to deal with influential movers and shakers from different environments. Here's how to become the go-to person in your chosen niche.

- Join professional associations. There is an industry association representing every market every market.
- Subscribe to the newsletters and journals in that market. Every market has specialized newsletters and journals and articles that are regularly published.
- Develop relationships, both professionally and personally, with centers and influencers that service your market. These are non-competing

professionals that comprise accountants, lawyers, bankers, and financiers, who also cater for the marketplace that you serve the same type of client as your familiarity and expertise within a niche market increase.

As your confidence and ability improves you will build trust with potential prospects, it will become easier to gain appointments, easier to market yourself, and easier to position yourself in within your niche markets.

Effective niche marketing comprises of two elements the markets that you focus on and a well-thought-out marketing plan targeting a few specific markets. This is not a numbers game, it's quality over quantity and it's a focus strategy.

Penetrate niche markets by holding and preparing for leadership roles within trade associations. This requires several months of active participation to gain visibility. Certain leadership roles such as treasurer, membership, even president, and serving on committees will give you the opportunity to give something back and learn even more about how industry works and meet potential new clients.

Other ways

- Look to take part at a local and regional, national level.
- Donate to your office.
- Hold social functions.
- Entertain clients and centers of influences.

It is a clear sign you've built trust and rapport within the target market when members regard you as one of them. In the financial services space, I'm considered an insider, one of them even though I don't operate a financial services business. I achieve this by understanding how the market works and the industry dynamics.

> For a long time, our primary market was local government authorities. About five years ago we acquired a company called Church Resources in New South Wales. We now have a significant footprint now in the not-for-profit sector. We have also started to sell a little bit into the private sector as well.
>
> (Joe Arena, CEO, Procurement Australia)

Another part of becoming the go-to person is your reputation. When you develop your reputation, you will minimize the amount of rejection received when marketing and prospecting.

The final strategy of becoming the go-to person in your marketplace is by employing a mix of promotional activities that fit within your comfort zone.

Raising your profile

Here are five ways to raise your profile in your chosen niche markets in niche markets:

- Planning niche market seminars – these can be full or half a day.
- Writing for targeted publications – start with a column and expand out to articles.
- Speaking to targeted groups – listeners will be a captive audience and many of the associations are continually on the search for speakers that can speak on a topic that addresses issues that concern their members.
- Identifying and attain membership in viable organizations. start by contacting your existing clients and ask about the associations they belong to. Sometimes this is something you should know, anyway. Ask for an introduction.
- Building a relationship with the executive director and board of your association.

Four key objectives when penetrating niche markets in developing opportunities:

1 To become active, visible, and serving the membership.
2 Create a favorable awareness of who you are and your range of services.
3 Stimulating inquiries from high potential suspects.
4 Paving the way for gaining acceptance when you make a warm outreach.

Use these objectives when preparing your niche market plan.

Top performer perspective

Kylie Stephens, Rural Risk Specialist

How did you discover your niche market?

I grew up on a cattle station, and I'm very comfortable dealing with farmers. I also ran an irrigation business several years. I enjoy helping people solve their challenging situations with their farms. The rural market is a natural fit for me. I understand their needs and special challenges and I enjoy working with them to develop solutions to their most pressing risk needs.

View from the field

The most effective way to market is to identify the markets you want to focus on and then develop a well-thought-out marketing action plan. A niche marketing plan is focused on a small number of niche markets. This makes it easier to obtain referrals and get appointments with prospective clients. A niche marketing strategy is narrow and deep while working from your comfort zone. Find one to three niche markets that you enjoy, develop your expertise and you will no longer find marketing to be a chore. It will become the standard way that you do business.

If you have other professionals working for you, niche marketing uses business time and resources effectively.

Key takeaways

- The key to predictable growth is to be seen as someone special, the special group of people.
- The first step to do this is to identify the markets you want to focus on. You cannot be all things to all people, and you certainly can't be all things to all clients.
- Every market requires a high level of expertise and experience to capture it effectively.
- Choosing an industry niche market(s) is one of the most strategic decisions you can make regarding the long-term viability of your business and your growth path.
- When you develop your reputation, you will minimize the amount of rejection received when marketing and prospecting.

Chapter 15

O – Observational marketing

Paying attention to your market

What is observational marketing?

Personal observations are an important and often under-used part of prospecting (Chapter 16) technique of paying attention to what's going on around you and in your market. Your observations comprise what you hear and read, providing insights and knowledge to identify trends, ideas and knowledge of suspects, and the information you can use to develop these into prospective clients.

Observational marketing is like being a good detective, getting the facts, and having the patience to fill in knowlege gaps to help you approach and land meetings with prospective clients by leveraging your insights.

What are the advantages?

Wayne Gretzky is a former professional ice hockey player who has been called the greatest hockey player ever. He is the leading goal scorer, assist producer, and point scorer in the National Hockey League history. When asked how he could score so many goals, he said, "A good hockey player plays where the puck is. A great hockey player plays where the puck is going to be."

Using your observations in selling helps position you to win early by playing where the market is going. You can spot opportunities and ideas (Chapter 9) early in the conceptual and get there before the competition. Early in my sales career selling commercial insurance, our firm heard about proposed changes to the worker compensation laws that we're going to eliminate coverage traveling to and from work under the law. I made several inquiries with employers and unions to discuss the impact. We developed an insurance program to fill this gap and successfully captured a share of this market well ahead of our competitors.

On a typical day, professionals follow social media, read newspapers, greet your neighbors, grab a coffee on your way to work, and have a friendly

DOI: 10.4324/9781003364580-16

chat with business owners. You may observe amenities with everyone you encounter, such as "hello," "How are you?," "How's business?," and "How's the family?" These can become more than just polite words when you develop your observation skills and awareness, and many times they can provide valuable marketing clues.

What are vation sources observation sources?

Here are seven observation sources that top professionals use:

1 LinkedIn
2 Newspaper
3 Newsletter
4 Industry trade publications
5 Business publications
6 Clubs and associations
7 Trigger events

LinkedIn

LinkedIn is a business and employment-focused social media platform. Professionals use LinkedIn to build and expand their professional networks. Once you've established your networking connections (you should have a minimum of 250–300), use notifications to stay updated on what's happening, such as promotions, new roles, and change of positions that could signal a need for your offering.

Newspaper

Help improve your general knowledge (Chapter 11) by reading your local newspaper in print and online daily. You can help you discover dozens of prospects and leads and opportunities.

Newsletters

There are thousands of newsletters available about any industry category. Subscribe to the ones that make sense for your niche market and industries.

Industry trade publications

A trade associations produce annual reports, newsletters, and journals for every major industry. Many of these are available online, and from your local library.

Business publications

Wired Inc, Harvard Business Review, and *Forbes* magazines are excellent sources for news, trends, and ideas. Many of these publications are available online.

Clubs and associations

Becoming active in service clubs and business associations such as Rotary and chamber of commerce can help you with building your network and tap into what's happening. When I attend my local business club, I engage with staff and fellow members.

Trigger events

These are changes within a business, industry, or market that could signal a need for your offering. Here are 12 common types to observe:

1 Change of ownership
2 Mergers, spinoffs, or acquisitions
3 Profit announcements
4 Winning new customer
5 Receiving an award
6 Expanding into new markets
7 New appointment
8 Resignations
9 Restructure
10 Important new product or service announcements
11 Downward spiral in business
12 New legislation

Top performers continually ask, "how does this create a need for my offer?"

How do you record your observations?

Track your recording by using a notebook or digitally. I recommend digital as it provides easy access with your computer, phone, or tablet. Recording options include:

• Drop box
• Evernote
• Notion
• One note

- Apple notes
- Read later app for websites and newspapers

What is record, listen, and investigate?

Developing a 24-hour awareness: when you observe something that you feel may be useful, follow these steps:

- Use active listening (Chapter 12) to observe (eyes and ears).
- Record what you find and discover.
- Investigate how you can use this information in your marketing.
- Read with a pen in hand.

Note down these names, and you can add them to your follow-up observation techniques.

Develop a 24-hour awareness

Know who will make a potential client. For example, if you've helped a client solve a problem with your offering, there is a good chance that others in the sector (competitors) could be experiencing similar issues. Leverage your client relationship to ask questions and investigate until you have located a hot-button need.

Use observation to learn new skills

This method of learning consists of modeling another individual behavior, attitudes, or emotional responsibilities. This is the way children learn. As salespeople, we can do that by observing others in our office, how other professionals approach their marketing, and get appointments to obtain referrals. That is how you develop good sales habits (see Chapter 8).

I know of an insurance professional specializing in the construction industry who gained a lot of intelligence and insights by simply observing as he drove to work, he would osbserve a vacant block of commercial land being surveyed, that was an indication that construction of a commercial building was being planned, which alerted him to a possible need for construction insurance.

To profit from your observations, ask the following questions:

- Can this information help land a meeting with the prospective client?
- Does this make sense?
- Is this he right way to proceed?

Another way to profit from observations is by engaging and exchanging pleasantries and polite small talk such as:

- How are things going?
- How's business?
- How's the family?

The answers may provide clues to identify a suspect, possibly a prospect just by being there, being in the moment. As you observe, you can determine what specific needs do they have. Once you know enough about a prospect, you'll be able to approach them under favorable circumstances to land a meeting to share a few ideas (Chapter 9).

How do you track what you learn?

Get in the habit of tracking changing situations and needs in your market. Record these on your phone, tablet, or computer. Create a niche market folder on your laptop and anytime you come across information in your niche market, save it there. Review your folder weekly and action any items that are worth pursuing. As your observation skill improves you will start noticing trends, developing ideas that you can share with clients and prospects in your niche markets.

Top performer perspective

Ward Dedman, CEO, EBM Insurance

What are you observing from your clients?

Our clients want and need a specialist risk sort of analysis, support, and advice. That also flows onto what insurers are chasing too. If you just present things in a vanilla sort of fashion, you will get a vanilla outcome. You must present a client's risks as a unique sort of set of circumstances, instead of a cookie cutter style attitude and approach.

View from the field

The habit of observation is a powerful and effective marketing method that only minutes per day. With dictation technology, it's never been easier to record what you see and hear on your computer or mobile devices. Once a week have your recordings transcribed; when you review, you might just find some gems that are worth pursuing.

Key takeaways

- Personal observations are an important and often under-used part of prospecting.
- Observations marketing is like being a good detective, getting the facts, and having the patience to fill in the gaps to help approach and land meetings with prospective clients.
- Your observations comprise what to hear and read, providing insights and knowledge to identify trends, ideas, and knowledge of suspects, and the information you can use to develop these into prospective clients.
- Using your observations in selling helps position you to win early by playing where the market is going.
- Pleasantries can become more than just polite words when you develop your observation skills and awareness, and many times they can provide valuable marketing clues.

Chapter 16

P – Prospecting

Getting meetings with prospective clients

What is prospecting?

Sales prospecting is at the heart of business development and the master skill of top professionals. It's also a learnable skill. It's the begging of your sales process where you search for, contact, and engage with individuals that match your ideal client profile.

Why is prospecting important?

To the surprise and frustration of many professionals transitioning into selling, prospecting is the lifeblood and getting profitable new clients in your target market is the key to both survival and long-term profitable growth, especially during turbulent times.

Even if you are getting repeat business and unsolicited referrals from your existing clients, there's about a 20% turnover in all accounts and increasing competition. You cannot always rely on this business, so becoming efficient at prospecting is a vital skill.

There are three types of prospecting approaches:

1 Traditional
2 Consultative
3 Client-centered

Traditional prospecting

Let me tell you about our company because I know about what I do more than you do and my job is to tell you about my company.

DOI: 10.4324/9781003364580-17

Consultative prospecting

I see my job as using questions and listening skills to learn more about you so that I can figure out the need that I can meet, with my capabilities and my services.

Client-centered prospecting

My job is to proactively share my insider's knowledge of success and proposing value-added solutions. I have accumulated and codified my experience in your niche and have distilled this into an action program to meet your needs. I understand the business conditions that are driving the market needs in your business and marketplace.

"Client-centered" is the approach for top professionals selling business-to-business intangible services.

What are the different prospecting approaches?

There are several ways to prospect. We will discuss five proven techniques that work and should form part of your marketing tool kit:

1 Email
2 Influencers
3 Social media
4 Referrals
5 Telephone

Email prospecting

This is an efficient way to work within your comfort zone. Email has a lot of advantages. It's fast and accessible, most businesses have email and you can easily reach and contact a prospective client. Email is easy to fit into your day.

Sending one or two emails per day to prospective clients and following up with a phone call, which we'll discuss in time management (Chapter 23), is a good strategy. Effective email marketing is about using brief paragraphs and sending customized handcrafted individual messages and not mass emails.

Four-step prospecting email format:

1 Establish credibility addressing a hot-button issue in your first paragraph.
2 Pique their interests.

3 Communicate your value proposition or cite results or ask a question.
4 Soft close, inviting them in a nonthreatening way.

Emails have a less formal style of writing than letters. Every message needs to be:

- Personalized to a business need
- Short and pithy
- Conversational

Email marketing permits any professional to work from their comfort zone. You can send and respond to emails from anywhere, your office, home, or on the road. Cold calling is unpleasant and in today's market is also unprofessional. A well-written email is an ideal way to warm up a call by setting the stage for a follow-up phone call. This is the quickest and most effective way to start a direct outreach strategy.

The sole purpose is to make a connection and then follow up. Most buyers spend time during their day writing or responding to emails and some block out certain times of the day, whether your prospect is traveling in their office, there's a good chance you can reach them quickly with a good, personalized email, and if the email addresses a hot-button issue that's on top of mind they will be very responsive.

Telephone prospecting

The phone very much still has a very valid place in the marketing arsenal. For example, you can often get passed gatekeepers calling a prospects cell or direct office number.

Most of us have mobile phones today. Telephone can be an effective tool for marketing.

Cold calling a prospect by phone is a tough business; before setting up your phone calls, first develop a scenario that could visualize the probable situation in which you'll reach out to the suspect business for looking at their needs.

- Who's directly responsible?
- What are the negative consequences of acting on your recommendation?
- What are the positive consequences?

The ideal way to use the telephone for the busy professional and to work within your comfort zone is to combine it with email to grab a prospect's attention with a

When contacting a prospect, you want to choose a hot button or important need that your target suspects want to solve. This increases the likelihood of them having a brief conversation with you.

These are brief conversations to set up a longer meeting. Focus on the need and the benefits you provide rather than pitching your product or service.

Find a need that is important enough for a prospect to meet with you.

What is social media prospecting?

The fundamentals of marketing and selling have not changed in the last 75 years, and I predict they will remain the same for the foreseeable future. Using social media is one unique aspect of technology that enables professionals' to prospect efficiently and effectively and, work from your comfort zone.

The best-known social media sites include Facebook, LinkedIn, and Twitter. These have allowed the seller today to increased the reach to their target markets. For prospecting, LinkedIn is the most powerful social media tool for establishing business connections. For example, I'm a frequent user of LinkedIn and I currently have over 1,200 connections directly connected to me, providing hundreds of thousands of indirect connections to people.

LinkedIn is about increasing the number of people you know so that you can gain access to the people you don't. When you connect with someone on LinkedIn, that's the equivalent of asking a client if you could access their computer or phone contact list of people you would like to know.

You need to build a LinkedIn connection between 200 and 500, which provides the critical mass to really take advantage of its resources. Commit to getting connected to as many people as possible to extend your reach and potential to meet new prospects and obtain referrals from existing clients.

Top performer perspective

Kylie Stephens, Agriculture Risk Specialist

How do you prospect for new business?

I receive many leads via word of mouth. My firm is well known in the agriculture community and my clients feel comfortable passing my along my name to other farmers in the area. We also have an extensive retail branch network that provides a huge range of products and services. I have developed several centers of influences with our retail branch network, providing me with a steady stream of new leads and opportunities.

Is there anything you would like to improve?

I would like to become more proactive in asking for referrals instead of waiting for clients to provide unsolicited referrals.

View from the field

Prospecting starts the sales process and the acquisition of new clients. Learning how to prospect is a skill that will serve well throughout your career. Professionals who master in prospecting are always in high demand. In its highest form, prospecting is referred to as rain-making professional service organizations.

Key takeaways

- Sales prospecting is at the heart of business development and the master skill of top professionals.
- Prospecting is the lifeblood and getting profitable new clients in your target market is the key to both survival and long-term profitable growth, especially during turbulent times.
- There are five proven techniques that work and should form part of your marketing tool kit.
- For prospecting, LinkedIn is the most powerful social media tool for establishing business connections.

Chapter 17

Q – Questions

The other side of listening

What are sales questions?

Sales questions help you find out what's going on in your buyer's world. They are the secret weapon of top professionals and knowing how to ask the right type of questions at the right time will help you uncover opportunities, prospects, cross sell, and close sales.

They help you connect with buyers, understand their needs, understand what's important to them, create better futures for themselves. Questions help you disrupt a buyer's thinking and change ceptions of what's true and what's possible to move the sales process forward, avoiding pitfalls that can derail a sale along the way.

Why are questions important?

The questions you ask can be more important than anything else. Prospects may not believe statements you make; however, they will certainly believe their own answers to questions being considered.

The ability to ask provocative and insightful questions is essential, especially in complex solution/intangible sales. Great sales questions help you win more sales. For service professionals, the skillful use of questions is the primary method for qualifying prospects and determining if they're a suspect or a prospect and if it's worth proceeding. They work hand in hand with observational marketing techniques (Chapter 15).

Questions help you find out what's going on in the minds of your buyers, their world and better understand their needs and achieve the following outcomes:

- Develop rapport
- Discover aspirations
- Demonstrate impact
- Define new reality
- Generate new insights

DOI: 10.4324/9781003364580-18

People do things for their own reasons and questions are the best way to help people state their own needs in their own words. Before you can do anything with a prospective client, you must establish credibility and trust both verbally and nonverbally; good questions help you get there.

"We like to engage with our clients by asking where are they going? What's worrying them? What is keeping them awake at night? Where do they see market heading?", says Ward Dedman, CEO of EBM Insurance.

Questions afford the opportunity to get in tune with a prospective client to find out where they are emotionally and intellectually heading, understand their language (Jargon, Chapter 10) – the words and phrases that are meaningful as well as those that are unfamiliar to them – to avoid misunderstanding, and provide them a greater sense of participation in an interview.

When used with skill, questions are an excellent way of giving recognition your can make people feel important and let them know that you respect their opinions.

What are the best type of questions?

Like any skill, your questions will improve with practice. Start by getting into the habit of asking questions in all your interpersonal contacts with friends, family, relatives, and colleagues.

Asking questions requires a skill, and it's more important to be mentally alert for potential needs and to be skilled in probing for needs than it is to be a smooth talker.

You earn the right to ask questions first by first asking permission, you reduce defensiveness by explaining why you're asking the question.
There are three types of questions:

1 Open-ended questions
2 Close-ended questions
3 Leading questions

Open-ended questions

Open-ended sales question is a question with no definitive answer, aimed at prompting a longer or more insightful response from a buyer. These questions are further divided into broad and specific questions.

Broad open-ended sales questions get people to open up and start talking. They're great for helping you find out what's going on in a prospect's world and are essential to sales success.

Examples of broad open-ended sales questions include:

"What's going on in your world these days?"

"Can you give me some background on what's happening in your company?"

Specific open-ended sales questions are more exploratory. Some buyers might not share much information when you ask broad open-ended questions, or they might not know the answers. These questions uncover latent needs the buyer might not even be aware of.

Specific open-ended questions yield one of three answers: an expression of need, no perception of need, or lack of knowledge.

Examples of specific open-ended sales questions include the following:

"You've mentioned that you'd like to improve your company's efficiency. There are a lot of ways to go about this. Let's start with billable hours. How closely do your monthly actual numbers align with your projected numbers?"

"What about staffing? Do your current employees have the skills needed to move the company forward? Where are the knowledge gaps?"

"What would you like to be doing that you just don't have the resources to tackle right now?"

Close-ended questions

These are sometimes called directive or fact-finding questions, answered with a "yes" or "no." Use closed questions to gather facts, start a conversation, gain attention, and draw people out of this to elicit preferred answers and a clarifier point.

These are great for diagnosis. Whether you get a "yes" or a "no" answer, it's easy to follow up and get the buyer to elaborate. By asking close-ended questions, you can uncover needs that buyers may not yet perceive as a problem, but when you ask so specifically, they sometimes reconsider.

Good questions give prospects a greater sense of participation in a sales interview and, when used with skill, questions are an excellent form of giving recognition.

Example of close-ended questions:

"Do you feel you're hiring the best people fairly consistently?"

"Are you getting the pool of candidates you want when you're looking to hire, and are you getting them fast enough?"

"When you make offers, do the best candidates accept them as often as you would hope?"

Leading questions

Elicit responses that confirm a preconceived idea or notion and push the respondent to answer specifically. Using leading questions helps you get meaningful information from a prospect, which helps him or her to determine if an offering is right for the prospect in question.

Leading questions allow professionals to guide the prospect toward making the right purchasing decision in his or her favor. Top professionals craft their sales leading questions by emphasizing the value of their offering and help a prospect see how the offering meets his or her needs.
Examples of leading questions:

- Having a solid insurance plan is important, don't you think so?
- When would you like to subscribe to our premium software package?
- How soon would you like to begin?

How do you prepare sales questions?

First, understand your objectives. If you know what you want to accomplish, it's easier to design your questions. Asking questions is establishing a relationship and the skillful use will help keep things on track.

Statements can be turned into a question by tagging them with "isn't it?" For example, this is a new opportunity for your business, isn't it?

Top performer perspective

Kathleen Beck, Mortgage Banker

What type of questions do you ask when working with a prospect?

I ask about their goals and dreams, and I don't talk about rates. Once I have an idea of what they are looking for, I can figure out how much they'll have to put down and how much their payment would be based on the sales prices or if they'll have to take their sales price down a little bit. It's just old school that we used to do. What payment do you want? And then let's move backward from there.

View from the field

Questions, observations, and listening go hand in hand. The ability to ask good questions can identify suspects and qualify them into prospects. Insightful questions help you build and maintain an overflowing sales pipeline filled with qualified prospects. When you first meet a prospect, ask good questions to learn about their situation, frustrations, challenges, goals, and expectations. The prospect should be talking 80% during this time, good questions are the key.

Plan your questions in advance, determine what you need to know, and write out your questions. Don't wing, instead carry your list of questions with you during sales meetings with prospects. Continue to ask good questions of your existing clients, don't assume. Your questions should be part of your service delivery to expand your client knowledge and create win-win relationships (Chapter 23) with your top clients.

Finally, good questions distinguish you from product-focused competitors, allowing you to concentrate on establishing long-term relationships.

Key takeaways

- Sales questions help you find out what's going on in your buyer's world.
- They help you connect with buyers, understand their needs, understand what's important to them, and create better futures for themselves.
- Questions help you disrupt a buyer's thinking and change a buyer's perception of what's true and what's possible to move the sales process forward.
- The ability to ask provocative and insightful questions is essential, especially in complex solution/intangible sales.
- If you know what you want to accomplish, it's easier to design your questions.

Chapter 18

R – Referrals

Leveraging existing relationships

What are referrals?

The most efficient and effective ways to generate leads and new business is by leveraging your client relationships. You get referrals in one of the two ways: passively when a client has passed your name to someone they know and proactively with a systematic approach to leverage your relationships.

In a prosperous market, too many professionals rely on casual referrals, passive leads, and luck to grow their business. When luck runs out, they wind up a poorly filled sales pipeline and have to rely on ad hoc and often unpleasant prospecting activities.

Why are referrals important?

A referral is worth 20 times over a cold new lead. Referrals are the most powerful method for attracting and landing businesses. A systematic referral approach is the backbone of a successful new business development program to maintaining an overflowing pipeline of qualified high-potential prospective clients. Building and maintaining an active referral program enables you to contact preconditioned prospects, who are more receptive to meeting because of the high regard for the referral person. It provides the following advantages:

- Selling from your comfort zone
- Increase your average revenue per client
- Lower the cost of business acquisition
- Improve client retention
- Reliable method for creating an endless chain of new leads

When I speak with professionals about how they generate new business opportunities, the answer most commonly given is through referrals.

DOI: 10.4324/9781003364580-19

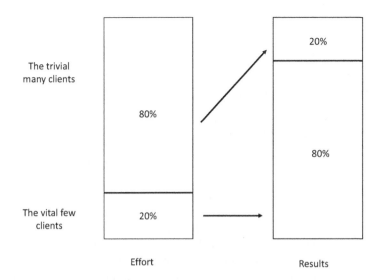

Figure 18.1 The 20% that matters.

However, most of these are passive referrals when someone has passed their name along to a friend or colleague.

Referral marketing is an efficient and effective way to market and sell your offering. Top professionals generate 80% of their new business from proactive referrals by following a client-focused system they know so well and can use it without thinking about it. They don't wait for their name to be passed along. Instead, they focus on helping their loyal to help them. Proactive referrals follow the 80/20 process as outlined in Figure 18.1.

People like to refer business and you actually do it yourself already when you tell someone about your favorite restaurant, dentist, mechanic, and so on. Top professionals make it easy for their best clients to help them with education on the types of clients they enjoy working and periodically reminding them.

What are referral relationships?

There are five types of referral relationships that you can leverage to generate a steady stream of leads and opportunities:

1 Client referrals
2 Non-client referrals

3 Niche market referrals
4 Strategic alliance partners
5 Personal network referrals

What are client referrals?

There is no activity that is more effective than an organized referral process to your existing clients. If you follow a disciplined client-focused process and are in frequent contact with your top clients, you will provide great service. You are in the right position to generate referrals, but only if you ask them.

A study conducted by Advisor Impact showed that one of the primary reasons clients refer is as an "act of reciprocity" for the good work their advisor has done. Another reason is that someone periodically reminds them and has a referral discussion with their clients at least annually.

The key is having a consistent referral process with the top 20% of your clients. Build this into your unique service model (Chapter 19) as a reminder to educate your best clients about the people you enjoy working with.

Follow these steps to generate leads and introductions:

1 First, ensure your clients are happy with your service.
2 Ask your clients to express this in their own words.
3 Educate your clients about types of people you are looking for.
4 Ask their advice on people they are connected to such as their LinkedIn connections.

What are non-client referral sources?

These are professionals and associations who serve the types clients you would like to attract for your business, including but limited to:

- Accountants
- Lawyers
- Bankers
- Real estate

If you develop ten non-client referral sources and you meet quarterly, obtain three referrals per quarter from each one, that is, 120 new leads per year. If you have a 50% conversion rate, that is, 60 new clients while working from your comfort zone.

What are niche market referrals?

These are key players within an industry niche respected by prospective clients, including:

- Market analyst
- Competitors
- Gurus
- Editors of publications

Meet with niche market key players every six months, educate, and exchange ideas and market intelligence. This should be a win-win relationship (Chapter 24) mutually beneficial for both parties.

What are strategic alliance partners?

These are formal referral relationships you have with other individuals and organizations who are serving your niche market. Alliance partners often include suppliers when you agree to collaborate on a project or marketing endeavor. An insurance carrier may collaborate with an insurance brokering firm to offer a product to a market segment.

Annually meet with your alliance partners to update each other about your ideal clients and exchange market intelligence.

What are personal network referrals?

Networking is done in two ways: formally, through networking groups, and, informally, through your own contacts staying on their radar screen. LinkedIn is an excellent tool for building and organizing your personal networks. Regularly contact them to provide updates on your value and educating on the clients you enjoy working with.

What is a referral mindset?

One of the most common reasons why many professionals do not ask for referrals is a discomfort and fear. They feel like they're crossing the line from a professional to a salesperson. However, a healthy mindset is that you believe prospective clients are not currently being taken care of, and it's your professional mission to ensure and make a positive difference.

The most common responses that clients will give when asked for a referral "no one comes to mind right now, but if you want to increase your referrals, you must help your clients to help you by reminding everyone that you've built your business on referrals. A healthy referral mindset is:

- You are offering or helping your clients rather than asking or selling.
- Assuming that most people in your niche market have a need.
- Your professional mission is to make a positive difference.

What is referral seed planting?

Promote your referral process to clients and everyone you know by reminding them that you are building a referral-only type of business. Referral seed planting follows the farming principles of sowing and reaping:

- You sow first then reap
- You only reap what you sow

Top professionals generating most of their new business via referral understand and apply the principals of sowing and reaping. Planting referral seeds is how you can use these principles in your business:

- Always acknowledging the importance of referrals with new clients.
- Reminding clients that primarily work on by referrals.
- Telling clients that you want to earn the right to know who they know.
- Letting clients know that you are never too busy to see a friend or colleague.
- Letting clients know that referrals are a natural part of the process when working together.
- Sharing your vision for your business.

Figure 18.2 presents a systematic referral approach to use with clients and referral sources.

If you actively and systematically focus on generating leads through referrals, you will always do well regardless of market conditions and the economy.

Top performer perspective

Kathleen Beck, Mortgage Banking Professional

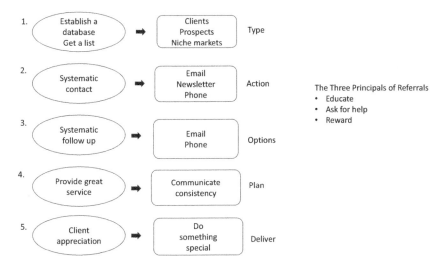

Figure 18.2 The five-step referral process.

Where does most of your business come from?

Over 70% of my new business is generated from referrals from existing clients and network partners. I have a large client base that I keep in touch with as well as centers of influences I've developed over the years from my network group.

View from the field

The goal for every service professional should be a 100% referral-only business. Get into the habit early of educating, asking, and rewarding your clients for referrals. By "rewarding" I mean keeping them in the loop and saying "thank you." Clients are happy to refer; however, it's up to you to educate them on who you are looking for providing a suggestion and following up. Referral marketing is an ethical and professional way to market and sell. When you leverage your existing clients for referrals, you are working 100% in your comfort while driving new business growth.

Key takeaways

- The most efficient and effective marketing for generating leads and new business is by leveraging your client relationships.

- In a prosperous market too many professionals rely on casual referrals, passive leads, and luck to grow their business.
- A referral is worth 20 times over a cold new lead.
- One of the most common reasons why many professionals do not ask for referrals is feeling of discomfort and fear.
- If you actively and systematically focus on generating leads through referrals, you will always do well regardless of market conditions and the economy.

Chapter 19

S – Service

Your process for turning prospects into clients

What is a unique service?

It is a custom-designed sales process based on your insights, wisdom, and understanding about your clients' hot-button issues. It's the core of your client-centered approach (Chapter 3) and when you package and execute this in your desired markets, you are better able to better sense, serve, sell, and satisfy the needs of your top clients, which will encourage them to use more of your service offerings.

You create your unique service from the information from client issues, requirements, and their aspirations to ensure that you never lose touch with your clients. Their needs and goals separate you from your competitors.

A unique service offering is a competitive advantage based on the needs of the client who uses them and not on the needs of your firm or the financial goals of your business.

Why do you need a unique service?

Your unique service allows you to develop breakthrough relationships to attract and keep high-end clients to your business, removing you from the commodity trap of product and price which is easily copied by competitors. It is your intellectual property (IP), the core of your marketing process.

Your unique service should focus your attention on developing breakthrough relationships with your top clients, categories A and B clients, that make up most of your revenues, and any category C clients with future potential for upgrading.

The bottom 80% of clients usually account for just 20% of your overall revenues. Some of these clients should be delegated or removed. Annually review the bottom 10 to 15% of your clients and delegate those out of your business order to someone else. Once a year upgrade your category B clients – this is the middle 15%.

DOI: 10.4324/9781003364580-20

Identify any that may have a potential for additional services you edu-cate them. Finally, look for catergory C clients and determine whether they have potential for upgrading.

How do you design a unique service?

Design your services by thinking from your ideal client's point of view. The components required are:

1   Creating a name
2   Prepare a need scenario worksheet
3   Outline the service components

These will become your source of competitive advantage.

Client-centered process

Use the worksheet shown in Table 19.1 to think through the components of your service and offering. Use this to describe how a client's condition will be improved by working with you.

Table 19.1 Service offering description

Improve or enhance	Reduce, relive, or eliminate
Decision making	Cost
Profits	Recurring problems
Appearance	Blockage to staff development
Internal operations	Excess capacity
Long-term outlook	Waste
Competitive capabilities	Risk

Protect	Restructure
Reputation	Unprofitable operations
Independence	Unnecessary reporting
Assets	Branch operations
Proprietary information	Organization
Self interest	Planning process
Security of products	

Identify-Develop	Restore or Resolve
Strategies	Long-term outlook
Key problem areas	Management structure
Decision factors	Outdated skills
Unforeseen opportunities	Market penetration
Solution to problem areas	Market competitiveness
Needs	Profits

This should to be the driving force behind the marketing of your firm and its offerings.

How do you name your unique process?

Your goal is to create a name for the key solution you provide that positions you in your chosen markets and defines the core value benefit. For this you need to:

1 Understand what you sell
2 Know your ideal client
3 Know your niche market

To generate ideas for your service name, jot down the names of services advertised in the publications serving your niche. Stay alert to the opportunities to rearranging and reshuffling various service names you see.

Example of names:
The Diagnostic Risk Profile
The Growth Finder
The 90-Day Check-up System
How do you outline the components of your offering?

Use the worksheet below to prepare a need scenario worksheet

The Need Use the niche market jargon or buzzwords (see chapter 10) to state the need as clearly and simply and powerfully as you can.
Key players 1. Direct players – who is the likely buyer within your target who is responsible? 2. Others involved – Who else may be involved in the decision-making process?
The consequences 1. Negative consequences – Of not proceeding? What risk and cost are associated with it? 2. Positive consequences – What benefits will the client receive from going with your offering?
The goal What is the goal or outcome?

The Sales Meeting

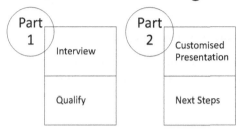

Figure 19.1 The sales meeting.

How do you present your service?

Your unique service should consist of two parts (Figure 19.1):

1 The initial appointment
2 Customized presentations

The initial appointment

The initial meeting fires off the starter's gun for a race, it starts the entire sales process. This can be face-to-face, virtually, or by phone depending on your selling situation and environment. This initial meeting should be for 30–60 minutes and achieve the following objectives:

Objectives:

- Building rapport
- Gathering information
- Qualifying
- Gaining commitment for second appointment (if qualified)

Setting the stage
Begin with a brief introduction and let the prospect know your agenda. Here is a sample script:

Sample script
"Mr Prospect, thank you for taking the time to meet with me today. I'm looking forward to learning more about your business and seeing how I might be able to assist you."

"The purpose of our meeting today from my standpoint is to get to know you better and learn as much as I can about your current situation. The best for me to accomplish that is to ask you some questions."

Use fact finding questions to interview and qualify the prospects (the gap analysis interview questions at the end of the chapter will help you with this). The goal is to look for a fit.

Closing the meeting
Thank the prospect for their time and willingness to share information. Restate your confidence that you can add value, suggest a second meeting to present your thoughts and recommendations.

Send a follow-up email:
Thank the prospect and reconfirm the follow-up appointment.

Follow up phone:
If you are unable to confirm a second meeting, use this script.
"Mr prospect this Joe Smith with Acme, thank you for your time and agreeing to see me yesterday. Based on the information you provided there are a couple of suggestions that I want to give you that make sense."

Briefly share the idea
Discuss a time to meet

How do you covert prospects into clients?

The second meeting
In part two, of your process is the sales meeting to covert a qualified prospect into a paying client. This meeting can range from 60 to 90 minutes. This a customized presentation showing how your offering will improve the prospect's situation, from the information and facts gathered during the first meeting.
In the presentation give an overview of:

• Your continuation process – how you work with your clients.
• Value – Packaging your offering to solve and/or address their hot-button needs and issues.
• Tools – The tools and resources you will use and provide to the clients.
• The next steps – Should include any deposit, signing of an agreement or letter of appointment to get things rolling.

What is nurturing?

Many prospects will not become clients during your first or second meeting. You will need to be patient, not everyone will be ready or able to do business straightway. In some cases, in can take 6, 12, or even 18 months to close a new business client. In these instances, the prospects will need to be nurtured so you remain on their radar screen.
This can be accomplished with:

- Sending out a monthly newsletter
- Inviting them to your seminars
- Sending articles
- Research reports
- Presenting new ideas
- Invitation to in-house events and networking opportunities

Each of these contacts provides valuable information and acknowledges the prospects' interest. Many of their existing providers may have stopped doing these types of things if they ever did at all. Selling is about relationships; most prospects and clients know there is often very little difference between competitors when it comes to the product and service offerings. When you take the time to follow up, you are creating breakthrough relationships.

Top performer perspective

Allan Manning, Founder LMI Group

What's an example of unique service you offer?

We invented policy comparison because it's just impossible for insurance risk professionals to stay up to date on different policies. We have 25 people full-time just reading policies, updating them. We do 1,000 plus changes a year in the policies. There are over 3,000 policies on the site and a thousand changes plus a year. The cycle is every three years and when new legislation comes through.

Insurance underwriters themselves send us their policies, if a broker gets a policy from an underwriter and it's not there on our site, they'll send it to us and within a week or two we'll have it up for comparison.

View from the field

To stand out from the crowd you need to create a unique service that addresses a client's hot-button issues by packaging your ideas and insights. This should be on your website and form the foundation of your marketing and prospecting activity.

Key takeaways

- It is a custom-designed sales process based on your insights, wisdom, and understanding about your clients' hot-button issues.
- You create your unique service from the information from client issues, requirements, and their aspirations to ensure that you never lose touch with your clients.
- A unique service offering is a competitive advantage.
- Your unique service should focus your attention on developing break-through relationships with your top clients.

Chapter 20

T – Time management

Getting stuff done

What is time management?

You have a limited amount of energy – the number of hours you work each day is less important than how many of those hours are productive.

Time is all a professional has, and how you use that time and your energy determines your success. Business success or failure doesn't just happen to you; it's all about choices about what you focus on and how you maintain that focus. David Mullen writes, "The right activities lead to the right results."

Top professionals spend up to 80% of their available time on sales-related activities. This includes gaining, developing, and keeping high-potential clients. Nothing is more important than your business, than your focus on these areas, and if you take care of these core issues, you'll experience what is possible.

What are the time management fundamentals?

You need to balance client time, marketing, and administration every day. Top professionals organized themselves by following and practicing four fundamentals:

1 Prioritize
2 Delegate
3 Block
4 Prepare

By following these fundamentals, you can get everything done that is necessary to have a successful career.

DOI: 10.4324/9781003364580-21

How should I prioritize?

Prioritize your most important activities first when your energy is high. Reading and research are tasks that are easy, but not as important as contacting prospective clients and building relationships.

Priority 1 – Monthly contact with clients (2–3 hours per day).
Priority 2 – Existing and new prospects (1–2 hours per day).
Priority 3 – High-priority admin task you cannot delegate.
Priority 4 – Admin, return phone calls.

Top performers constantly reevaluate and prioritize to ensure that they are spending 80% of their time on sales-related activities.

Use the remaining 20% time to complete admin and other stuff. During prime time selling, manage the continuation process for your categories A and B accounts, generating most of your revenues. Delegate the bottom 80% of your clients to your assistant to handle the routine transactional work. I've worked with several top professionals managing seven-figure revenue portfolios, the top 20% of their accounts consist of 40–75 relationships that they manage following a client-focused continuation process during the year.

They guard their time to deliver a high level of service and in return they are rewarded with high-quality referrals that keep their sales pipelines flowing with high-potential prospective clients.

What is the morning/afternoon system?

You do your high propriety activities (Big 3) in the morning – before, avoid the temptation of responding to emails and other activities during this time. It takes discipline to avoid looking at emails and other stuff that may divert our attention away.

Use the afternoon to do your admin – follow-up calls – prepare anythings outside the "Big 3."

If you follow this system, you will be spending 50% of your time in proactive activities to grow your business and career and still have time to handle the reactive activities to get done.

What is delegation?

You must try to delegate everything that is not involved with building client relationships and getting in front of new prospective clients. You oversee your portfolio of clients, however; you do not need to do every task. Build the checklist and follow through.

If prioritized properly, you should be able to handle ten high-priority admin items per week. If there are more than ten, chances are that you are probably not delegating properly.

Here are the things you cannot and should not delegate:

- Resolving operations problems that an assistant cannot
- Client or prospects presentations
- Following up
- Unresolved client problem
- Preparing a presentation
- Top client review

Schedule 1 hour per day to handle two issues.

Keep a sheet of paper and track items that are not under the big 3 – delegate these to someone else.

What is time blocking?

Time blocking is a process to help you maintain your focus. It opens the door to achieving high accomplishments in your calendar. If it doesn't get scheduled; it doesn't get done. The simple act of scheduling tasks on your calendar instead of writing them on a to-do list will force your mind and reduce stress.

Focus on making sure that key things are get done.

All professionals have a choice. They are either in business or in busyness. Most average professionals "are in busyness"; they do not focus their time on what really needs to be done.

Time blocking is focusing to get your 20% key activities done, focusing your time on similar activities for a period.

Time blocking is a process, a system to help you maintain your focus. It permits you to concentrate productive activites activity and high accomplishment. Nothing is more important to your business and career than your focus on developing relationships with prospects and clients.

The real challenge lies in honoring the system that you have by protecting the time you've set aside and using it with an absolute focus in the face of a barrage of interruptions and false priorities.

Time blocking is a skill that, when learned and practiced, will become a key productivity habit, and will become, over time, one of the most important business habits you'll ever gain – performance.

Top performers prioritize activities according to their ability to make their business grow and block the time in their calendars to ensure they have the time to do it.

They first take care of your marketing and lead generation. Only when these important things are done that they turn their focus on other important activities.

Top professionals don't have to-do list; instead they have a have-to list and use time blocking to ensure that the have-to list is done before the to-do's.

They know what must happen at the beginning of each year, month, week, and day by scheduling a chunk of time for everything else that's important.

Schedule a chunk of time for everything that is important, that is, prospecting. Follow up, nurturing existing clients and client relationships.

Schedule important items as early in the day as possible. Reschedule them if necessary. Treat your time blocks as if there were appointments.

Avoid busyness

When you give every activity equal importance, prioritizing happens only when deadlines and problems force you to react to them.

Develop a process-based business machine all that is required is for you to switch it on each day. Examples of process include:

- Continuation process – existing client contact
- Prospect first appointment meetings – questions to qualify
- Pipeline management
- Account checklist
- Follow up
- Objections/problems answers

The goal is to execute your vision and have all the processes in place to execute this seamlessly.

What is living in your calendar?

Average sales professionals use to-do lists, which is like children picking at their food by starting with their veggies, starting with their favorites, and saving the veggies for a last time, by which time they get to them they are cold, and you don't feel like doing it.

In selling, some professionals fall into the busyness service trap. They believe that only they can serve their clients and they have no time to sell, with prospecting becoming a low priority.

Until your goals hit your calendar, you won't consistently hit your goals. Aside enough time to accomplish the activities that will drive your business to the highest potential. Don't fall into the service trap, instead hold yourself accountable by focusing your energy on when you must do it.

You have a choice. You can either be in the busyness or business focusing 80% of your time on sales-related activities.

The important trait is knowing how to focus on the most important thing and how you're going to get it done.

Top performer perspective

Richard Crawford, CEO, CBN

How do you block out time to get stuff done?

We have a typical planning structure, at the highest level we have some strategic goals, which are set three years out. They're now not that far away and they've been pretty much the same for that time. Annually we reset based on what's happening around us, our view as to what we must achieve in the year, and then quarterly we review that. We try and end up at the beginning of each month with some key milestones and objectives that we must hit at each quarter.

It's easy for us to get lost in the day-to-day traffic. We talk often about balcony and dance floor; we must actively make time to get on the balcony. To do that you've to consciously choose between things we do and don't do. I have a weekly team stand-up with my team where we talk about what are our three priorities for the week; it's all about conscious choice the whole time as to where we focus our attention.

For me, it's a monthly target and I make sure that I'm allocating time not only for appointments, but also for governance papers, board papers, and phone calls. It depends on what we must achieve in the month or the quarter.

View from the field

Time is your most valuable asset and how you spend your time will determine your success. There are so many distractions and it takes a deep level of motivation and discipline to focus on the right activities. The right activities are the following:

- Appointments with new qualified prospects
- Follow up prospect meetings.
- Client meetings
- Getting referrals

You should spend the majority of your time doing these tasks.

Key takeaways

- You only have a limited amount of energy – the number of hours you work each day is less important than how many of those hours are productive.
- Top professionals spend up to 80% of their available time on sales-related activities.
- You need to balance client time, marketing, and administration every day.

Chapter 21

U – Upgrading
Staying sharp

What is upgrading your sales skills?

Top professionals continually update their knowledge and experience and use it to their competitive advantage. In every profession there are things you must know and accomplish for survival you have no choice.

Top professionals fully understand their value, ideal clients, and the ultimate benefit of their offering. They take charge of their learning and professional development.

Several years ago, there was a television game show called the $64,000 question where contestants answered general knowledge questions. With every successful answer, the money doubled and to the point where the final question was worth $64,000. A contestant who applied to go on was a psychologist. The producers initially knocked her back, the show was looking for someone with dramatic career juxtapositions, for instance, like a marine officer who is an expert cook or a shoemaker who knows about opera.

The psychologist started studying boxing until she became a boxing expert. She then recontacted the show's producers and said, "I'm a psychologist who knows about boxing." They threw every tough question at her and eventually she won the $64,000 question. She went on to become a very famous psychologist and her name was Dr. Joyce Brothers.

Why is upgrading important?

It's important to continually strive to update your sales and marketing skills including your knowledge on offering and value proposition. This help you identify new opportunities improve cross-selling and upgrading of existing clients, and overall improved retention.

DOI: 10.4324/9781003364580-22

Top professionals vieew themselves as self-employed regardless of if they work for a firm or for themselves accepting complete responsibility for their own learning. They take charge of their future by continually upgrading their training and education.

To grow you must keep yourself up in both knowledge (expertise) and the art of selling (training). Top professionals attend their local professional development workshops, association meetings, and conferences. They have a receptive mind and are smart enough to walk away with things to help them. You might gain something new from a speaker or colleague or might recall something you've forgotten.

What are the fundamentals?

The fundamentals of effective selling consist of knowledge, skills, and attitude as shown in Figure 21.1.

Knowledge

This is the science of your expertise: accounting, finance, engineering, and so forth, learning the technical aspects of everything you need to know. During the educational phase you learn what there is known about your field of expertise (technical knowledge), the product history, compliance, wordings, and the book of knowledge. Education is done in the classroom.

Skills

This is the art of selling, putting someone in the field in a comfortable way. The best thing about skills training is that anyone who is naturally bright and can learn anything and everything there is to learn would be successful. You can't master sales skills from just reading books; you learn and master it through practice, performing, and feedback.

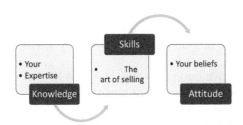

Figure 21.1 The three fundamentals of effective selling.

Attitudes

Your attitudes and beliefs define what you'll do and become (see Chapter 2). There is a story of a farmer who brought an unusual pumpkin to the country fair. The pumpkin appeared to be normal except for it was shaped exactly like a two-gallon drum. The farmer won a blue ribbon for it. When asked by a reporter about how did he ever get a pumpkin to look like that, the farmer said "It was easy, as soon as the blossom fell off and the fruit started to grow, I just stuck it inside a two-gallon jug. When it was ripe, I just broke the jug, and the sunshine did all the hard work!"

In a similar way our thoughts and attitudes shape us. Below are nine fundamental attitudes of top performers.

A good way to continually upgrade and keep your sales skills sharp is by completing annual audit or review of your sales skills and behaviors. Use the worksheet shown in Table 21.1 to rate your skills and selling strategies. Rate yourself on a scale of 1–10 in each area and ask yourself:

- What are your strongest areas?
- What are your weakest areas?

And create a plan to help you maintain your strengths and improve or correct any weaknesses – something that should be done on an annual basis. To upgrade your skills, you need to:

- Find a coach, teacher, or mentor to help upgrade your skills.
- Attend training courses.
- Listen to podcasts.
- Read books or build your library.
- Attend conferences, seminars, and workshops.

How do you improve your client knowledge?

There are seven categories of information you should know about each of your clients:

1 Contact information, name, email, website, and industry: the specific niche market they serve; some products they sell, who they sell to, and their business philosophy.
2 Customers: the number of active customers they have, the kind of data they have with their customers. What are their dream clients look like?
3 Salesforce: how many salespeople do they have – are they inside salespeople or outside salespeople? What are the strengths and weaknesses? What is their average order? Standards for hiring people.

Table 21.1 Sales skills audit worksheet

	Weak								Strong	
1. **Selling System** – You have formal sales process you followed.	1	2	3	4	5	6	7	8	9	10
2. **Prospect Pipelines** – You have an overflowing pipeline.	1	2	3	4	5	6	7	8	9	10
3. **Focus** – 80% your time is focused on sales-related activities.	1	2	3	4	5	6	7	8	9	10
4. **Preparation** – You practice and rehearse all prospect and client presentations.	1	2	3	4	5	6	7	8	9	10
5. **Relationship management** – You have a formal program in place to manage clients, prospects, partners, team members, and centers of influence.	1	2	3	4	5	6	7	8	9	10
6. **Referrals/Introductions** – 75% or more of new business comes from either a referral or an introduction.	1	2	3	4	5	6	7	8	9	10
7. **Account Development** – Goal is 100% full-time clients.	1	2	3	4	5	6	7	8	9	10
8. **Retention Strategies** – Formal review process for the top 20% of accounts.	1	2	3	4	5	6	7	8	9	10
9. **Centers of Influence** – You have ten centers of influence with quarterly face-to-face visits or interactions.	1	2	3	4	5	6	7	8	9	10
10. **Targeted Account Size** – You have a targeted account size for your sales pipelines.	1	2	3	4	5	6	7	8	9	10
11. **Specialist vs. Generalist** – You have identified that you have become or in the process of being a specialist.	1	2	3	4	5	6	7	8	9	10
12. **Value Adding** – Focus on providing value to the client, not just price.	1	2	3	4	5	6	7	8	9	10
13. **Qualifying** – You have a formal new business strategy in place for sales discussions.	1	2	3	4	5	6	7	8	9	10

4   Marketing,: what is their target market? What is their market potential? Do they market locally, regionally, or internationally?

5   Strategic partners: Do they have the alliance partners?

6   Professional background: their position, their goals, and how'd they get started?

7   Competitors competition profile: who are the competitors? The top three competitors?

- 8 Markets and industries:
- Creating a niche library of books, websites, and industry links. On your computer, setting up industry subject files on key topics. Organizing your CRM data information on clients and prospects. Selecting the best industry data sources for the niche market you wish to serve.

Top performer perspective

Mark Anderson, Barrister and Financial Services Legal Specialist

What is your market?

My niche market is bespoke risk advice usually for clients who are insurance focused. We not only provide them with insurance solutions and respond to disputes but also provide them with alternatives to insurance solutions.

How do you deliver value?

Value consist of time incurred and results also provided, complexity, client demands and expectations.

View from the field

Top professionals don't stand still, and neither can you. You must continually upgrade your skills to stay up to date and relevant. Create your own personal development program to keep your mind and skills sharp. Invest in your own learning and development and be willing to invest in courses, coaching, and mentoring.

Key takeaways

- Top professionals continually update their knowledge and experience to reflect on it and use it to their competitive advantage.

- It's important to continually strive to update your sales and marketing skills including your knowledge on offering and value proposition.
- Education and training are two completely separate things.
- The best thing about training is that anyone who is naturally bright and can learn anything and everything there is known to be successful.

Chapter 22

V – Value selling

How to avoid competing on price

What is value?

Products and services are largely a commodity in the eyes of clients and prospects. Price is a lousy way to compete. Top professionals focus on value and what is in their client's best interests. Having the best products and most flexible pricing is not enough in today's market.

Value is defined through the eyes of your client or prospect; however, your brand is a major contributing factor in helping you to build your value and clients like to be associated with success.

Prior to the rise of internet in the 1990s, all the knowledge used to rest with professionals. For example, to purchase an airline ticket you had to contact your local travel agent who would search the rate book, provide a quote, and issue the tickets. Today anyone with access to a computer can quickly access all the airlines to compare flight options, car rentals, and hotel accommodation.

What is a value-based mindset?

Selling has changed over the past few decades as access to the internet has helped buyers to become smarter and better informed by conducting their own research and analysis. Having the best products and most flexible pricing is not enough in today's market. Products and services are largely commodities in the minds of clients today, with so many choices and competitors in the market.

Harry Beckwith says that top professionals first sell themselves, their company, their offering and prices. Average professionals sell on price, their service, themselves, and finally their business. To become value focused, think in terms of the client's results and outcomes. Every client is trying to make money or save money. Consider the following questions:

DOI: 10.4324/9781003364580-23

How will they be better off from working with you?

How do you provide solutions that address their hot-button pressing needs?

Value is about results. For example, if value-based pricing were applied to the healthcare sector, they would pay a doctor treating a patient for a broken leg more if the patient fully recovered and less if the patient ended up with a slight limp.

The recipient always defines value, not by the provider. It's always rooted in their personal and organizational needs and experience with your offering.

How do you create a value-based approach?

Understanding your value is the first step to be effectively able to market your offering, to gain the attention, and attract perspective clients.

Questions to ask include the following:

How does your offering improve, enhance, protect, identify, reduce, relieve, eliminate, restructure, or restore something?

These are all verbs to help describe your value and identify potential benefits that accrue when applied to a prospect.

When you fully understand your value, it's much easier to position and market your services, get meetings, land appointments, convert networking into opportunities, nurture prospective clients, and get referrals.

There are seven key principles of value selling:

1 Do your research
2 Don't lead with your sales pitch
3 Ask questions (and listen)
4 Share your value
5 Teach, don't preach
6 Focus on the buying process, not the selling process
7 Be genuine

Do your research

Review a prospect's website, sales information, and use LinkedIn to obtain background information on your buyer, previous employment, and any common connections that may be able to provide you additional insights.

Don't lead with a sales pitch

Build rapport, use questions to verify information and details you've discovered during your research.

Ask questions (Chapter 17)
Use open-ended questions to build rapport and establish a relationship. Design several insightful questions and use your listening skills to learn about your prospect's needs and objectives.

Share your value

Discuss the outcomes and results that your offering provides to your clients.

Teach don't pitch

Take the time to educate your clients on what you do and how you do it.

Be genuine

Always focus on what's in the best interest of the client.

How do you present your value?

It begins with packaging (Chapter 16) and your value proposition, which is a brief statement that tells people who do business with you improve their condition.

A good value proposition is always outcome focused on the needs, problems, struggles, and challenges of a prospect and not your offering. Clients don't purchase your offering, your products or services. They buy your promise to work with them in creating a more favorable future as they define it.

There are four steps to achieving value-based goals:

1 Respond to the client's needs.
2 Use your knowledge to deliver value.
3 Provide constant client-focused service that leads to long-term retention of desirable clients.
4 Build value-based relationships with clients and make superior performance and client satisfaction the driving force of your business.

How do you present value in your proposals?

Make it easy to understand. Articulate your value and the success, remove tired superlative buzzwords. Use terms and phrases that clients instantly understand. Make each claim relevant to the client issue that you're currently facing.

For example, instead of promising an optimal solution for production errors, say

- "We will reduce production errors by 10% in 120 days."
- Use buzzwords and jargon in your proposals carefully.

Buzzwords to eliminate:

Optimal, fastest, shortest, easiest, least maximum and unsurpassed, best in class, best in practice, ground-breaking, enabler, leverage, real world, world class ramp up, etc. These commonly used words add nothing to your value.

Instead, fully define what your value means to a client and avoid using too many pronouns.

Instead of you know, such as we, us, me, may, and I, talk instead about your client issues, the issues and challenges that they're facing.

Value is the foundation on which you build your marketing. It begins and ends with results. To succeed, you must offer and deliver results and solutions. You must deliver undisputed value to your clients and everyone else in your network.

What is the value link?

It is the link between clients, prospects, and business comprising three client-focused marketing processes that require your focus, time, and attention. A client-focused marketing process is a set of activities designed to produce and deliver value to your target market. It's all about acquiring, keeping, and developing your desirable clients while you work within your comfort zone (Figure 22.1).

Acquiring link – The acquisition of new clients comprises prospecting and personal selling, including:

Prospecting – Finding qualified suspects and contacting them for a meeting to discuss one or more of their needs and personal selling, face-to-face new business discussions you plan to conduct with clients and prospects.

Retention link – Managing, shaping, and exceeding client expectations using your continuation process (Chapter 3).

Figure 22.1 The value link.

Development link – Providing additional services and selling more to existing clients, developing new revenue, and leveraging existing client relationships to gain new ones.

The value link is your unique value adding factors that create breakthrough relationships. This is your proprietary X-factor (Chapter 24) tool; your competitors easily duplicated an intangible non-purchase.

Top performer perspective

Joe Arena, CEO, Procurement Australia

How do you convey your value to a client?

This is a good question whenever we get a new salesperson that they grapple with "what's the value that we deliver"?

There are several things; first and foremost, the one that has been tried, tested, and found true over a long period of time is our governance frameworks. Government agencies are not allowed to engage with a supplier unless they go through a government compliant process themselves.

Two state governments went through a due diligence process and determined our go-to-market strategy had robust governance framework and would stand up to probity. So much so that they said "yes" to local government working through Procurement Australia, that's a strong value proposition in time and cost savings.

View from the field

Price is a terrible way to compete; someone can always come up with a cheaper price. Focus on developing and fine-tuning your process, asking good insightful questions, and focus on what is in the best interest of your client. Dedicate yourself to becoming an expert in your chosen niche market and leverage existing client relationships to acquire and build new ones. When do your homework, you are bertter prepared and able to educate clients on your value.

Key takeaways

- Products and services are largely commodity in the eyes of clients and prospects.
- Price is a lousy way to compete. Top professionals focus on value and what is in their client's best interest.
- Value is defined through the eyes of your client or prospect.
- Value is the foundation on which you build your marketing. It begins and ends with results.
- Average professionals sell on price, their service, themselves, and finally their business.

Chapter 23

W – Win-Win

The ethical way to sell

What is a win-win?

Win-win is the mindset of top sales professional to satisfy both your business and client outcomes. The client feels that they received a good deal and the business achieved a good return for the time, energy, and resources invested. Figure 23.1 outlines the four outcomes of a sale.

Category 1 – The business and the client are happy with the outcome and there is the possibility of a long-term mutually beneficial relationship.

Category 2 – High business satisfaction and low client satisfaction. The business is happy with the price and profit margin. However, client is unsatisfied and may leave for a competitor.

Category 3 – The client is satisfied but the business is unhappy as it takes a loss because of a pricing discount.

Category 4 – Both the business and client are unhappy immediate corrective action is required.

Why is win-win important?

The mindset of seller vs. prospect does not work anymore and is adversarial. Today's buyers are smarter, more sophisticated, and knowledgeable than ever and can make their own decisions between competing products and services without the help of a sales professional. They are looking for long-term partnerships.

A win-win relationship is the key to maximizing retention, lifetime value of clients, and generating referrals.

Today, more than ever, businesses are operating in a low switching cost environment because they focus on selling on price and when prices drop, clients switch. Mortgage providers sell the lowest rate and when interest

DOI: 10.4324/9781003364580-24

Win Win Model

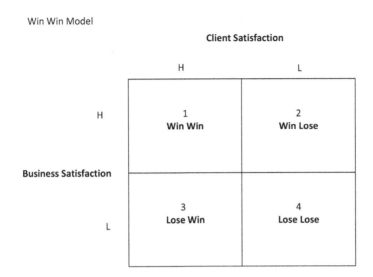

Figure 23.1 Four outcomes of a sale.

rises, client's move to the next person offering a cheaper rate. Insurance brokers focus on the cheapest premium. When premiums rise, clients shop around for someone who can offer a cheaper rate. When you only focus on price, the cost of change/switching is not as painful for the client.

Business-to-business (B2B) firms and individuals, including real estate, finance, insurance, advertising, and banking, practicing these methods are struggling to compete on price in a low switching cost highly competitive world.

Price is a commodity and a lousy way to compete. (Features, benefits, and price-focused clients cannot differentiate between you and a competitor – you are simply a commodity.]

A win-win relationship mindset and approach are an ethical way to do business. It's about delivering value, focusing on the self-interest of your five key relationships.

Providing value is a better way to compete and differentiate your offering. Top performers objective is a win-win relationship delivering satisfied clients, repeat business, becomes easier to get and generate a steady stream of referrals, maintain an overflowing pipeline filled with qualified prospects.

How do you create a win-win?

The seller brings a win-win mindset. It's the way you do business, including the following elements:

1 Be willing to walk away.
2 Be selective with client acquisition.
3 Stay in control.

Be willing to walk away

Be prepared to walk away from poor business that does not stack up. You can always want to win a client, but you don't need to. Establish conditions when you will walk away, including:

• Clients who are argumentative
• Dishonest
• Unethical
• Unpleasant
• Won't work collaboratively

Be selective with client acquisition

Take business on your terms. Not all business is good business. Categorize your clients to identify the top 20% generating most revenues to help you identify your ideal clients. Don't hesitate to cull problem clients.

Stay in control

Create a checklist of your ideal client conditions, your values, and your selling philosophy. Take the time to qualify and learn prospect's objectives and ensure that there is a fit. Develop a meeting agenda to share this with clients and prospects, summarize sales meetings and mutually agree on next steps.

There are generally five reasons a prospective client won't buy or do business.

1 No need
2 No money
3 No desire
4 No urgency
5 No trust. The big one!

Figure 23.2 Prospect zones.

What are buyer zones?

Prospective clients fall into one of the three zones as shown in Figure 23.2. You will make a sale when they are in zone 2 actively seeking a solution or zone 3 that has a pressing need.

To build a win-win business, you need:

- A successful client-focused sales process
- A value offering that delivers incredible results to help clients achieve their outcomes and improve their condition
- Skills and capabilities to ask questions and build relationships
- A good sales philosophy and concept

As we explored in an earlier chapter, your client process makes the individual client or a high-potential prospect in a targeted market the beneficiary of your specialized knowledge, resources, experience, and information.

Is win-win ethical?

A win-win mindset is an ethical way to sell its partnership selling.

The Yellow Pages was for many years the primary advertising method for a small business. The prized procession was the right in your niche category. The salesperson would often use fear tactics when a buyer raised objections. If someone hesitated to renew their advertisement or questioned the price increases, the salesperson would tell them if they did not renew their advertisement position they would go to their competitor. There was very little relationship building, many clients fell into category 2 Win Lose. Today the Yellow Pages is a shadow of its former self and is struggling to survive; as other cost-effective alternatives became available, businesses quickly switched to these often without having to engage face to face with a salesperson.

Prospects do not buy from people they dislike or trust.

The goal is to achieve a win-win outcome. You are well rewarded for your efforts and your client walks away with great value, and price is not the driving force.

What are objections?

Objections are a natural step in the selling process. Be wary of a buyer with no objections at all; he might have them and not be sharing them with you. When you view objections as a necessary step toward gaining commitment, they are less likely to derail your sale.

Nearly all objections boil down to one of the four types mentioned below:

1 Lack of urgency
2 Lack of trust
3 Lack of money
4 Lack of need

Lack of need

A buyer does not yet perceive, or does not yet admit, the need to solve a problem.

When a buyer says there's no need for what your offering will solve, it may be true. But it's also possible that you are not resonating or not addressing the right need. Or they simply don't see the value in what you offer.

Guidelines to handle objections:

• Focus on outcomes, not process.
• Ask good questions to uncover needs.

Objection number # 1 lack of urgency
Uncover and communicate rational impact. Build the return-on-investment case this requires estimating numbers and doing math. Let the buyer choose and compute the numbers so that they can get the solution. The buyer must see a tangible dollar value.

Guidelines

• Help the buyer see the tangible benefits
• Uncover the emotional impact

Objection # 2 lack of trust
The buyer needs to believe that you can do what you say you'll do. You need to establish your credibility.

Guidelines

- Prepare relevant stories and examples.
- Be genuine and show interest.

Objection # 3 lack of money
This is probably the most common objection. You can overcome price and get full fees for your offering.

Guidelines

- Make sure it's a money issue.
- Make sure you are speaking with the decision-maker.
- Work to uncover the real objection.

Objection # 4 lack of need.
Use questions to properly qualify the prospect before presenting or recommending.

Guidelines

- Spend the necessary time establishing a relationship and qualifying.
- Stay in touch with prospects who are not ready to buy yet.

Top performer perspective

Robert Kelly, CEO, Steadfast Ltd

How do you create a win-win relationship?

I realized that we are only as good as our relationship with the insurer we act for. And if we don't make them money and we make money, then it's not a very good relationship. We have 29 underwriting agencies, for the most part they've stayed with their capacity providers and we have taken remedial action on pricing to ensure that we could get through it.

It is important to understand the circle you operate in and ensure that nobody in that circle has been disadvantaged or taken advantage of if you want that circle to stay intact. Our success since 1995 (the year we started) has been based on the fact that we are cognizant of all the players that provide us with the ability to get revenue, and we ensure for the most part that we do the right thing by them, and that we don't look to take advantage. I look for consistency in relationship that's sustainable rather than quick fixes that you take advantage of.

View from the field

A win-win relationship with clients is a sure-fire way to building a great career and lifestyle. Selling becomes easy as you seek and create partnerships. You build your own proprietary network by creating breakthrough relationships, high retention, and steady streams of referrals. Whenever you have dealings with your clients, you both should walk away feeling good about.

Key takeaways

- Win-win is the mindset of top sales professionals.
- Today's buyers are smarter, more sophisticated, and knowledgeable than ever and can make their own decisions between competing products and services without the help of a sales professional. They are looking for long-term partnerships.
- A win-win relationship is the key to maximizing retention, lifetime value of clients, and generating referrals.
- Objections are a natural step in the selling process. Be wary of a buyer with no objections.
- Nearly all objections boil down to one of four types:
  - Lack of need
  - Lack of urgency
  - Lack of trust
  - Lack of money

Chapter 24

X – X factor

Developing your personal power

What's an X factor?

Selling is a mental game. To succeed, you need mental strength and personal power. The "X factor" is what makes you unique that your clients can only get this from you. It is the human dimension to selling.

Selling is a hard work. To be successful, you need to be tough enough to deal with continual rejection, potential failure, disappointment, setback, and obstacle.

People will buy from you because they like and trust you. Your attitude toward yourself will reflect their attitudes toward you. Sales skills, product knowledge, and education account for 20% of your success. Thoughts, feelings, attitude, values, goals, and self-image account for 80% of your success (Figure 24.1).

What about optimism?

Research conducted by Professor Martin Seligman from the University of Pennsylvania found that sales professionals who scored high on optimism sold 37% more than their pessimistic counterparts. Sales professionals who tested in the top tier in optimism had 88% higher sales production than those who had scored high in pessimism.

Seligman's research also revealed that those salespeople who had pessimistic mindsets were 300% more likely to quit the profession of selling than those who were optimistic.

Why is an X factor important?

This is your competitive edge, the way you conduct your business, build relationships, and solve problems. It is your key benefit that is not easily copied by a competitor. It's what makes you and your business unique.

DOI: 10.4324/9781003364580-25

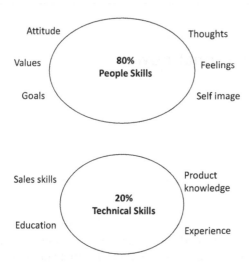

Figure 24.1 Human dimension.

All top professionals have an X factor. It's the way they go about their business, solving problems, identifying challenges, and helping clients achieve better outcomes. You X factor is about building a memorable persona to get people are talking and mention you to others.

X factor is team work.

I used to be the vice president of sales for an outsourcing company. When I was looking to expand my support team, I advertised internally and discovered a young man, A. Rocket, working on the help desk, who showed great potential as a pre-sales consultant. The role suited him perfectly. He found his X factor and became my team's go-to person for major key accounts. They often heard me saying, "Get me the Rocket" – today he has successful career today working for a major bank.

Admin people keep getting jobs in admin but if they could see themselves as experts in information retrieval experts, a whole new world and opportunity opens up for them.

What are the X factor elements?

There are seven elements required to master the inner game of selling and developing your personal power:

1 Taking a long-term view
2 Result thinking
3 High energy

4 Grit
5 Agility
6 Self-control
7 Critical thinking

Taking a long-term view

Before his magical National Football League NFL)career began, Tom Brady played college football at the University of Michigan from 1995 to 1999. For the first two years, he was the backup quarterback to Brian Griese, who too was a future NFL quarterback. Brady's first-ever pass for the Wolverines was an interception.

He was the seventh quarterback taken in the draft taken in the sixth round and the 199th overall pick by New England Patriots. The scouting report on Brady at the time wasn't too kind. He failed to impress scouts as they considered him to be slow, while also lacking the powerful arm to disrupt a defense. Over 23 seasons, we regard him as the greatest NFL quarterback.

Top professionals are not born salespeople. It takes time to master and hone your sales skills, develop a niche and sales capabilities. Having a long-term view about your career for five years or more means you will invest the time, energy, and resources required to become a top professional.

A big reason I was drawn to insurance was the major 1998 Katherine Floods.

I was 17 at the time and living in Katherine when the flood hit

The entire town went under which including my family home with just the roof showing.

We lost absolutely everything apart from the clothes on our backs that day with no one expecting the river to peak as high as it did. For this reason, items like precious photos, videos etc. were all destroyed in the flood so even today there is not many photos of my childhood nor mum and dad in their early years.

I remember rows and rows of beds at the Katherine high school which is where my family had to stay until we were able to try and get accommodation at a hotel where my cousin worked.

Anyways to cut a very long saga short, I remember going to see the local insurance company with my mum to try and sort out a claim for our house. I remember everything about the lady that was trying to help us and how insurance helped rebuild the town.

I got to see at an early age just how important insurance was and the emotion surrounding level of cover, sums insured and at a time of crisis

you really do not want to sitting there with regrets. Insurance has fasci-
nated me from that day forward, and the Katherine floods has a big role.

(Kylie Stephen – Risk Specialist)

Result thinking

Top professionals see the ends before the means (see Chapter 5). Top professionals don't need to know how they will achieve a goal before setting it. Avoid goal setting inside a box that is only as big as their present
knowledge.

I was often given me sales growth targets that I initially felt were unreal-
istic. I did not now know how I was going to achieve the growth numbers
that were being asked of me. I learned early on to set the goal – focus on
the result. After a while I started noticing opportunities, identifying suspects, converting those suspects into opportunities and eventually into
new clients.

High energy

Selling is a hard work that demands high energy (see Chapter 26). Top
professionals have energy. They know you can't be your best if you don't
feel well.

They do regular exercise at the gym or take part in their pursuit, e.g., running, squash, or organized sport. They eat well and get plenty of rest. They
take the time to recharge their batteries with breaks and vacations to stay
fresh and on top of their game.

Grit

Grit is a personality trait possessed by individuals who show passion
and perseverance toward a goal despite being confronted by significant
obstacles and distractions. Those who possess grit can self-regulate and
postpone their need for positive reinforcement while working diligently
on a task.

Agility

Agility means the ability to get up to speed quickly and learn fast, and
acquire new knowledge and skills about a prospective client, industry, or
market.

Self-control

You feel good about yourself to the degree to which you feel in control of your own life. You understand you are the primary creative force and the law of cause and effect, that there is a reason for everything that happens.

Critical Thinking

You create your own system of success. Alan Weiss says, we learn in "conscious competency" and incorporate success regularly by making such learning "unconscious." When combined with agility, information processing is a learnable skill, based on asking the right questions to generate the right answers. Too people ask the wrong questions.

How do you find your X factor?

The late Joe Gandolfo regarded as one of the ten greatest salespeople in the United States and the number one insurance agent in the world. Joe's X factor: he specialized in estate tax and gift planning for affluent clients. Joe processed each of the seven essentials: strong work ethic and commitment, combined with his niche market focus on developing a thriving and successful career. Your abilities are as unique as a fingerprint, understand them and.

Ask yourself:

1 What makes your business stand out?
2 How do you offer clients the most value?
3 What is your business great at?
4 What makes you stand out individually?
5 What could your X factor become?

Top performers approach their role from an attitude of being self-employed, and this was mentioned earlier, being in charge of their own destiny, accepting total responsibility for everything that happens to them.

Top performer perspective

Bernie McIntosh, Managing Director, Victorian Mortgage Group

What is your X factor the one thing you do better than anyone?

We are providing a phone service, an ease of contact when a broker has a hot opportunity to take to the marketplace, they can give us a call and we will give them an immediate response as to whether we can help them or not. They know quite confidently if we do say "yes," we will back that up and set the transaction for them. It's that ease of phone service that we offer that I think is critical for us.

View from the field

Finding your X factor takes time, but when you find it you will have a distinct competitive advantage. Selling is people and relationship business. Take the time to ask yourself the five questions. Get help from your family and friends. Your X factor can and should evolve and you grow as a professional and acquire new skills and expertise. Use the growth as a springboard to the next level, going after bigger clients and tackling complicated problems and issues that prospects are facing in your chosen markets.

Key takeaways

- Selling is a mental game. To succeed, you need mental strength and personal power. The "X factor" is your value.
- People will buy from you because they like and trust you. Your attitude toward yourself will reflect their attitudes toward you.
- All top professionals have an X factor. It's the way they go about their business, solving problems, identifying challenges, and helping clients achieve better outcomes.
- There are seven elements required to master the inner game of selling and developing your personal power:

  1 Taking a long-term view
  2 Result thinker
  3 High energy
  4 Grit
  5 Agility
  6 Self-control
  7 Critical thinking

Chapter 25

Y – You

Packaging your X factor

What is a personal brand?

Your personal brand is your product putting you in charge of your career. It is packaging your X factor qualities (Chapter 24) and communicating it to your ideal clients about what makes you special and unique. People buy from you first, then they buy from your firm's services and offering. Building a personal brand is essential to becoming a top performer.

Your brand is finding your story, Harry Beckwith writes, "Your brand is the truth about you, well told. Like every company, every person has a dozen good stories that reveal that person." A talent in marketing is to discover your stories that may have been forgotten, ignored, or overlooked – and tell them well.

Why is branding important?

Your brand can help you cut through the clutter in the marketplace, gain the attention of prospects, land meetings, acquire new clients, generate referrals, and expand your network and market reach. A strong personal brand propels you to the top of your niche markets, allowing you to become the go-to person in your chosen niche.

A good personal brand means being able to share with the world and your ideal clients about what makes you special and valuable for them. It's challenging and adventure discovering what makes you and your business unique and you may be pleasantly surprised.

Top sales professionals think like a CEO of their own business, they forget about the usual job titles and descriptions, and they are loyal to their clients, colleagues, and relationships. They act selfishly to grow, promote, and market themselves and add continued value to their clients.

William Bridges says you are the boss of your own career. Top professionals have a future-oriented perspective in their career and of the aspects of their life, they focus more than just on next year's numbers and targets

DOI: 10.4324/9781003364580-26

and your personal brand is your product that solves your client's problems. As your brand gains familiarity within your market, so will your confidence and ability to build trust with prospective clients.

How do you build a personal brand?

The first rule is be authentic. People trust brands because they are credible to be what they say they are. No one responds to our efforts to be other than the person sitting across from them. Building a credible brand begins with five questions:

1 What is your story?
2 What do you stand for?
3 What are you against?
4 Who are your ideal clients?
5 What is your offering?

What is your story?

To borrow one of the ancient slogans in advertising, "Your brand is the truth about you, well told." Everyone has unique personal experiences, work experiences, and achievements. To stimulate your thinking about what makes you unique, ask these questions:

- What are two to four things you know?
- What challenging current projects are you working on?
- What are you great at?
- What important new connections have you added to your personal and professional network?

Seek out of the help of your friends, family, colleagues, clients, and associates and list down your skills, education, and experiences.

List up to five core skills. You can mean you personally or your business.

What do you stand for?

List three things you stand for. These can also be "values" or "things you want to be known for."

1 Your craft/expertise
2 Helping people
3 Value based

What are you against?

List up to three things you are against. Try to solve these issues that exist in your niche market.

What obstacles have you faced?

List some obstacles you have had in your business journey. This can include personal issues if they've affected your business. For example:

- A problem with your industry or where you worked previously
- A struggle that will resonate
- An advantage you didn't have

What are your ambitions? Try not to make this about money.
For example:

- Self-focused
- Focused on others
- Overarching goal

Use your answers to the above questions to write up a summary. Get feedback from your friends, colleagues, and/or family.

Who are your ideal clients?

You cannot be all things to all people, find your niche market (Chapter 14) and describe your ideal client. Select no more than one to three niche markets and spend the necessary time for becoming an expert. Avoid being seen as jack of all trades and a master of none. Find your niche market and focus your message on the needs of prospective clients in that market.

Who do you enjoy working with – For example:

- Founders
- CEOs
- Company directors
- Business development
- Sales professionals

What market segments interest you? For example:

- Marketing
- Technology companies

- Manufacturing
- Retail
- Financial services

Where are your ideal clients located? For example:

- Worldwide
- Nationally
- Locally

What is your offering?

What pain points can you solve?
General pain points:

- Lack of new sales calls
- Lack of exposure

  "I love what I do, but I'm not a sales person"

Problems with existing solutions:

- Suppliers are expensive.
- Suppliers want to lock you into long-term retainers.
- Providers over-promise and under-deliver.

What pain points can you avoid?

- No long-term contracts
- No aggressive selling or practices

Tie these benefits to time, money, or reduction in stress.
 This becomes a clear statement of the tangible results a client gets from using your offering. When you express your value, it should be outcome focused, financially oriented, and speak about the issues your niche market is facing.
 For example:

- Less time needed opening opportunities -> More time to focus on clos-ing deals
- More sales calls/meetings -> More closed deals -> More cash
- More money -> Less stress with cash flow -> Greater capacity to profit and expand

Clients often cannot tell the difference between one firm's offering and that of another. When you approach a prospective client and meet anyone the first question you'll likely be asked is "What do you do?", you must answer this simply.

How do you put your brand to work?

More people fail as professionals because they don't have the self-management skill; they fail because they lack a good education or the right kind of experience. Top professionals understand well that their brand is their product. Your product is not your job title or description.

Your brand is a combination of your product, expertise, and knowledge. You put your unique brand to work in everything that you do. When you are prospecting, your unique brand helps you to land appointments and gain the attention with prospective buyers when you're putting proposals together. And when you're delivering, a unique brand helps you to close more sales and, more importantly, your unique brand is going to help you to generate referrals and develop good centers of influences.

When you have a unique brand that integrated in your sales philosophy, you're taking charge of your career and become an asset to your firm. If you're independant professional you have the freedom to set your numbers, to set your targets, to set your focus. You're charting your own course in the waters. You are choosing where you work, how your work and who you work with.

Whether you work independently, employ others in your own business, or work as an employee, it's you, your brand, that they're gaining the wisdom of your experience and expertise. Your brand, all the work you've done, is your value statement of how people are better off using your services. It becomes evident in your marketing messages and the fabric of everything that you do, and it becomes evident in the way that you service your clients.

Top performer perspective

Richard Crawford, CEO, CBN

The whole idea of taking control of your career is important and being clear on your purpose and what really energizes you. The best way to do that is to look back first before you look forward and ask what have been my best and most successful times and what has given me the most energy and joy in my life?

In that way you can work out where your strengths and interests lie going forward. It's about asking "how can I set my career?," "what are the sorts of things I want to be doing?," and "how do I develop my interests based on my strengths?"

If you want to do something to take control of your own life, you've have to basically start doing it now and don't wait for a catastrophe. We're all pretty good it certainly gathers our attention rapidly.

When someone has that conversation with you about career choices, it's best to be in control of yourself and have that conversation with yourself. It's the best thing I've ever done at different stages of my career, having the opportunity of talking to someone and getting some professional mentoring and guidance. If nothing else, it makes the reflection that you do so much more powerful.

View from the field

Don't underestimate the value and power of your personal brand. It's a culmination of everything you've done and experienced. Invest the time pulling the pieces of your career and personal experience together to tell your story in a unique way.

Key takeaways

- Your personal brand is your product and puts you in charge of your career.
- People buy from you first, then they buy from your firm's services and offering. Building a personal brand is essential to becoming a top performer.
- Your brand can help you cut through the clutter in the marketplace, gain the attention of prospects, land meetings, acquire new clients, generate referrals, and expand your network and market reach.
- Top sales professionals think like a CEO of their own business, they forget about the usual job titles and descriptions, and they are loyal to their clients, colleagues, and relationships.
- Top professionals act selfishly to grow, promote, and market themselves and add continued value to their clients.

Chapter 26

Z – ZigZag

How to recover from setbacks

What is zig-zag?

This is to take a sharp right or left turn due to an unexpected event, opportunity, or circumstances. In sales sometimes things do not always go according to plan; there are twists, turns, and detours; and you have to be prepared for the unexpected and think creatively to bounce back and stay on track.

Tammie Jo Shultz is known for being one of the first female fighter pilots to serve in the US Navy. Following active duty, she became a commercial airline pilot for Southwest Airlines.

On April 17, 2018, Captain Shults safely landed Southwest flight 1380 after an engine failure, with debris causing rapid decompression of the aircraft. One passenger was killed when partially stuck through a damaged window. Captain Shults safely landed the plane in Philadelphia.

Pilots practice in simulators so that when an actual event occurs, they will be fully prepared and ready to respond. Top sales professionals practice and rehearse their presentations, likely objections, asking for referrals and qualifying questions prior to visiting a prospective client.

Why is zig-zag important?

Sometimes the shortest route is not a straight line.

When Benjamin Franklin was working in London as the deputy postmaster general for mail to and from the American colonies, he asked his cousin Timothy Folger, who was the captain of a merchant ship, "why it took ships like Folger's so much less time to reach America than it took official mail ships."

Folger told Franklin that whalers knew about the "warm, strong current" and used it to help their ships track and kill whales. "In crossing it [we] have sometimes met and spoke with those packets, who were in the middle of it, and stemming [sailing against] it," however, the mail ships "were

DOI: 10.4324/9781003364580-27

too wise to be counselled by simple American fishermen," and kept sailing against the current, losing time as they did so.

A zig-zag is necessary due to an unexpected opportunity or circumstances. These can be both positive and negative events such as:

- The chance for a bigger sale
- Buyer (decision-maker) departs
- A merger
- Meeting starting late
- Change of ownership
- Internal change of strategy
- New competitor

You have no control over the unexpected but you can be ready and prepared for both good and bad. Becoming a top performer is simpler than you might think. Not easy just simpler. What I mean is what you need to do is clear and it's possible for anyone to do it. However, when I say anybody and can succeed, I don't mean everybody will.

The great thing about sales is that it's not about what everyone can do, it is about what you can and will do. It is about opportunity, not averages. Your future success depends on your ability to focus in the right direction. Your direction determines that targets you can hit. Top performers focus on the simple issues that make big things happen.

You may encounter clients, prospects, and colleagues who become roadblocks who simply do not understand how change affects markets and creates needs that can be fulfilled by people who know how to package your knowledge and expertise into a product that is your "X" factor.

Here are five simple steps to keep you heading in the right direction:

1 Create a personal plan.
2 Time block to get your focus.
3 Get accountability to keep your focus.
4 Make sure your environment supports your focus.
5 Keep your energy to maintain your focus.

Create a personal plan

Set high goals in key areas and focus on implementing your plans. Gary Keller says, "An amazing truth is that process bring[s] focus even when we ourselves feel unfocused.

When you focus on implementation, achievement of your plans becomes not only possible but also likely. Don't let your goals become ceilings, set goals that place the finish line away, give yourself time to catch your breath, and celebrate your progress. Stay focused on acquiring, retaining, and leveraging your clients and you will take your business to the highest possible levels.

Time block to keep your focus

Block your time to make things happen. Focus to make sure the key things are get done.

Time blocking is a way of budgeting your time (see Chapter 20) by setting aside to accomplish the activities that will build your business. Setting priorities, budgeting your time for your top 20% of activities, are key skills that must be learned and practiced, to develop good productivity habits. Time blocking is a process, a system to help you maintain your focus.

Get accountability to keep your focus

Use accountably to keep your focus (see Chapter 1). Accountability picks up where time blocking leaves off, by helping you to shape and reshape your focus, it's a learning loop. You get the best accountability through a relationship that follows a process that regularly refocuses you.

> I always create a listening space for my team, and I coach and mentor them and encourage them to tell me what's working as well as what's not. We build in time for fun every Friday for our nerve centre meeting.
>
> (Richard Crawford, CEO, CBN)

Check your environment

Whether or not you are aware of it, your business environment and personal environment matter. It must support your goals. The more you are aware of the power of your surroundings to affect your life, the sooner you can address it to take charge.

Your environment includes:

- Physical
- People

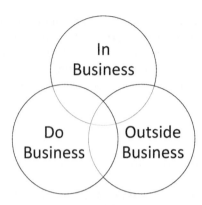

Figure 26.1 Your people environment.

Physical environment (productivity) includes your office, furniture, equipment, and tools for supporting your productivity goals. Either they are supporting your efforts to keep you focused or they are distracting you.

Your people environment which is about energy and synergy falls into three categories (see Figure 26.1):

1 People you are in business – These are your colleagues and the business you work in.
2 People you do business with – These are your clients, strategic partners, and suppliers.
3 People outside of your business – These are outside people including family, friends, and pastimes.

You are the gatekeeper; your environment can make or break you. Top performers don't leave it to chance, they shape, craft, and make their environment one that helps them reach their potential.

Energy

You cannot reach big goals without a big, sustained effort. Top performers are high-energy individuals. Figure 26.2 outlines the five energy areas.

Here are some energy ideas

1 Spiritual energy – Your thinking, reading, and meditating – read something positive to uplifting to begin your day.
2 Physical energy – Exercise and eating – going to the gym, running in the morning, and starting the day with a good breakfast.

Figure 26.2 The five energy areas.

3 Emotional energy – Laughing – Sharing a joke or story with your significant other before work.
4 Mental energy – Planning and learning – Spending 15–30 minutes in planning your day and calendar.
5 Business energy – Lead generation and client acquisition – Executing your daily plan.

Top performer perspective

Simon Swanston, CEO, ClearView
    I get my energy from developing people, I've worked across three continents and I'm very proud of the people I have developed.

View from the field

It's not if but when; unexpected things do occur in sales many times outside of our control, however we should be prepared. There are probably not many objections that you have not heard before. We get caught in traffic on the way to an appointment. Plan your day first in the morning, leave some wiggle room, in other words don't book back-to-back appointments.
    Being able to zig-zag is about remaining calm under pressure, being able to think and plan in the moment. Pay close attention to your environment – this can easily be underestimated. It's too easy to get caught up in office politics and negative when it might more sense to plan your day working from home and call into the office as required.
    The great thing about sales is that you can set the rules, you don't need to ask for permission to turn left or turn right; create your zig-zag to achieve your goals.

Key takeaways

- In sales sometimes things do not go according to plan; there are twists, turns, and detours; and you have to be prepared for the unexpected.

- Sometimes the shortest route is not a straight line.
- The great thing about sales is that it's not about what everyone can do, it is about what you can and will do. It is about opportunity, not averages.
- Your future success depends on your ability to focus in the right direction. Your direction determines that targets you can hit. Top performers focus on the simple issues that make big things happen.
- Becoming a top performer is simpler than you might think. Not easy just simpler.

Reading material

The following books are excellent resources and complement *The ABC of Professional Selling.*

Title	Author	Publisher	Date
Originals	Adam Grant	WH Allen	2017
Value-Based Fees	Alan Weiss	Pfeiffer	2008
Masterful Marketing	Alan Weiss and Lisa Larter	BLM	2022
Peak	Anders Ericson and Robert Pool	HarperOne	2017
Grit	Angela Duckworth	Vermilion	2017
Visionary Selling	Barbara Geraghty	Simon & Schuster	1998
The Big Books of Words that Sell	Bob Bly	Skyhorse	2019
The Power of Habit	Charles Duhigg	Century-Trade	2022
Financial Services Sales Handbook	Clifton Warren	BEP	2015
To Sell Is Human	Dan Pink	Text	2013
Getting Things Done	Dave Allen	Penguin	2003
Marketing Your Consulting and Professional Services	Dick Connor and Jeff Davidson	Wiley	1997
Phases that Sell	Edward Werz and Sally Germain	Contemporary	1998
Selling the Invisible	Harry Beckwith	Warner	1997
You, Inc.	Harry Beckwith	Business Plus	2011
Selling to Big Companies	Jill Konrath	Dearborn	2006
Contagious	Jonah Berger	Simon & Schuster	2013
Words that Sell	Richard Bayan	Contemporary	1984
Influence	Robert B. Cialdini	Quill	1993
Start with Why	Simon Sinek	Penguin	2011
How to Get a Meeting with Anyone	Stu Heinecke	BenBella Books	2018

Index

Note: Figures are indicated by *italics*. Tables are indicated by bold.

personal doughnut: impact on business
32; marketing model 31–2; meaning
of 29–30; organization model 32;
process of goal setting and 29; sales
model 30–1; service model 31
personal network referrals 105
personal plan, creation of 154–5
personal traits, of top performers *45*
pipeline 60
podcast and social media 51
positioning statement 60
presentation, importance of 43–4
pricing, value-based 129
proactivity, habit of 45
problem solving 89, 142
Procurement Australia 27, 47, 62
products knowledge 64
professional and personal
development, habit of 46
professional development 82
profit margin 61
proposal writing 57
prospecting 61; client-centered 93;
comfort zone approach for 95;
concept of 92; consultative 93;
discipline of 18; emails 93–4;
importance of 92–3; for new
business 95; sales 92; social media
95; telephone 94–5; traditional 92;
types of 93–5
pyramid of priorities 19

qualified lead 61
quasi-profession 11

raising the bar 32
ramblers, handling of 71
Reagan, Ronald 11
real estate 104
referrals: client 104; five-step process
107; habit of asking for 44;
importance of 102–3; marketing
103; meaning of 102; mindset
105–6; niche market referrals 105;
non-client sources 104; personal
network 105; seed planting 106;
sources of 107; strategic alliance
partners 105; types of 103–4
renewal revenue 54
request for a proposal (RFP) 57
results, tracking of 5

return-on-investment 24, 138
right mindsets, development of 10
Ron, Jim 18

sales: asking for 44; knowledge 63;
meeting *112*; methodology 61;
philosophy 10–11; worksheet **33**
sales process, choosing the right time
in 44
sales questions: close-ended 99;
importance of 97–8; leading 100;
meaning of 97; open-ended 98–9;
preparation of 100; right to ask 98;
types of 98, 100
sales skills audit worksheet **125**
Savage, John 64
segmentation of clients, by revenue
14–15
Seinfeld, Jerry 20
self-accountability 5–6
self-discipline: to achieve desirable
behaviors 18; approach to
implement 20; endless chain
concept 20; importance of 18–19;
law of familiarity 19; as learned
behavior 18; meaning of 18; pyramid
of priorities 19
self-organization 44
Seligman, Martin 141
service trap 5
social communication 54
social media prospecting 95
social selling 61
sound bites 61
Steadfast Group 11
Stephens, Kylie 84, 95
strategic alliance partners 105
strategic partners 126
Swanston, Simon 53, 157

target market 79–80
technical knowledge 123
telephone prospecting 94–5
three blind men, story of 8
time blocking 118–19, 155
time management 93; by avoiding
busyness 119; blocking out time to
get stuff done 120; concept of 116;
fundamentals of 116; living in your
calendar 119–20; morning/afternoon
system 117; prioritization of most